P9-DGL-588

Mary Keen

THE GARDEN BORDER BOOK

Photographs and plans by Gemma Nesbitt

Capability's
Books
Deer Park, WI
54007

First published in the U S A in 1987 by
Capability's Books
P. O. Box 114
Deer Park, W I 54007

All rights reserved

ISBN: 0–913643–02–5

Copyright © Mary Keen, 1987
Illustrations copyright © Gemma Nesbitt, 1987

Printed and bound in Spain by
Cayfosa, Barcelona

BOMC offers recordings and compact discs, cassettes
and records. For information and catalog write to
BOMR, Camp Hill, PA 17012.

FACING TITLE PAGE: *A woodland and wild flower border where a narrow path that seems almost too overgrown to walk down is mysterious and inviting.*

Contents

—

Introduction 8

1 Monet Colours in a Cobbled Herb Garden
John and Caryl Hubbard 14

2 A Bold Design for a Low Maintenance Border
The Lady Remnant (designed by Peter Coats) 20

3 A Warm Wall in a Cold Climate
Dr Edward Jarvis 24

4 An Architect's Water Garden
Jeremy Benson 28

5 Herbs in August
Rosemary Verey 32

6 A Handsome Shrub Planting
Mrs David Edwards 38

7 A Traditional Kitchen Garden Border
Mary Keen 42

8 All Year Interest for a Gravel Forecourt
John Brookes 48

9   UNUSUAL PLANTS FOR A SHADED WALL BORDER
Mrs Ralph Merton   52

10   EASY ALPINES FOR A CIRCULAR BED
Amanda Garmoyle   56

11   SILVER SHRUBS AGAINST A BRICK FAÇADE
Caroline Todhunter   60

12   A WEEKEND GARDENER'S BORDER
Edward Fawcett   66

13   AN APRIL TO OCTOBER BORDER
Christopher Lloyd   70

14   A HOT, DRY BANK WITH ARCHITECTURAL PLANTS
John and Caryl Hubbard   76

15   A COURTYARD GARDEN
Faith Raven   80

16   A FORMALLY LANDSCAPED BANK
The Hon. Mrs Alec Cobbe (designed by Lanning Roper)   84

17   A HIGH-SUMMER BORDER WITH UNUSUAL PLANTS
Mrs Hady Wakefield   88

18   AUTUMN COLOUR IN A GRAVELLED GARDEN
John Brookes   92

19   A TRIANGULAR BED
Leeds Castle (designed by Russell Page, modified by Stephen Crisp)   96

20   A SMALL SHRUB ROSE BORDER
Alvilde Lees-Milne   100

21 Leaf Forms and Shades of Green for Spring
Caroline Todhunter 104

22 Easy and Elegant Double Borders
The Hon. Mrs Alec Cobbe (designed by Lanning Roper) 108

23 A Collector's Corner
John and Elizabeth Parker-Jervis 112

24 Impressionist Colour in a Country-house Border
Mrs Gordon Foster 116

25 The 'Mingled' Border
John Sales 122

26 Winter Planting around a Tree
A. W. A. Baker 126

27 Golden Shrubs for a Dark Setting
Alvilde Lees-Milne 130

28 A Strong Colour Border
The National Trust at Lytes Cary (designed by Graham Stuart Thomas) 134

29 Old-fashioned Roses in a Modern Planting
John and Caryl Hubbard 140

30 Woodland and Wild Flower Border
John Codrington 144

List of Suppliers 148

Selected Reading 149

Index 150

INTRODUCTION

Gardening books abound. There are books for the novice gardener which explain how to grow all the plants in cultivation and books for the specialist which indulge in rare detail. There are other books written to describe the effects produced by associating one plant with another and books about the toils of 'making a garden', but even the best of writers cannot conjure up a complete picture of a flowerbed for those who are unfamiliar with Latin names and who probably have a rather limited repertoire of plants which they can recognize. This offering is an attempt to show people who come late and reluctantly to gardening how the assembly line works. It is for those who spend time and money on beautifying the insides of their houses and who cook delicious meals and mind what they wear, but whose gardens are often unplanned. It is for my friends, who are defeated by gardening 'because it is too difficult'. It is for those in despair of ever understanding how successful gardeners arrange their plants and for the people in a hurry who want instant effect. For all these it might be a beginning.

There are thirty plantings to choose from in various styles and settings. Many of the gardens from which they are taken are famous and all of them can be visited. Throughout the book there are examples of work by leading garden designers, including those who work for the justly famed gardens of The National Trust. There are also plenty which have been planned by gifted amateurs. Anyone who follows the advice carefully should end up with a passable imitation of a bed which has taken years of thought and a certain amount of trial and error to achieve. Rarely is a plan right first time and a good gardener is constantly changing things round, so the end product will never be perfect, but it will be a start. For some, selecting small sections of plantings will work better than making a copy; others may find that the general advice in all the written descriptions might make sense of something they already suspect. For the more experienced, I hope that the book offers a look behind the scenes in other people's gardens. Everybody recognizes that one of the best ways of learning how to combine plants is to go and see what others have done. The detailed analysis of plans should interest those who would not dream of copying the plantings in full (because they enjoy doing it themselves), but who are not above being intrigued by how the successful achieve their results. The choice of plantings has been governed by a desire to persuade people to look at their gardens with the eyes of an artist rather than with those of a horticulturalist. Knowing how to grow things is important if you want to make a garden, but not as important as people make out; it's

OPPOSITE: *A kitchen garden border contains traditional flowers like columbines, peonies, daisies and sweet williams.*

8

knowing where to put them that matters. The quick-sands of taste are tricky ground and the choice is bound to be personal. I like some beds much better than others, but recognize that there is a place for the sort which I would not want in my own garden, and I respect anything which does what it sets out to do – and works. There are shapes and sizes to suit all settings, and I hope that there is enough variety in soil, situation and mood to fit most people's needs.

SITE

The best place to choose is obviously the sunniest and most sheltered that you can spare, but shelter from wind is more important than sun, so concentrate on providing that first if you are on a wind-swept hill, otherwise you will never grow anything but low and wiry plants. Every house (unless you happen to live in one that is triangular) has a south-facing wall which can be pressed into service if nothing else seems suitable. Where the wind roars in from east and west, buttresses of yew or large shrubs can protect the corners and create a micro-climate. (Use wattle hurdles for instant shelter while you wait for things to grow.) Out in the open, garden walls and hedges still make the best background for traditional borders, but posts and wire with climbers trained to them will also provide backing. Island beds always threaten the feeling of space in small gardens, but there are places where they can look good. Big borders are easier to manage than small ones and both

are much less work when established than the weekly struggle with the lawnmower, so make the flower-bed as large as you dare. If the beds in the book are too long for your purposes it would probably be better to telescope the middle and miss out a chunk than to cut off an end, because there is a risk of ending in thin air if you eliminate the important plants at the edges. Preparing the soil is important, and if it means taking a year to eradicate serious weeds like ground elder or bindweed, then take it. There is nothing so tiresome as chasing the hydra heads of convolvulus, or painting individual leaves of elder all summer, while they steadily multiply among the expensive new plants. The weeds will always win, because under cover of other plants they can fight a guerilla war, only coming into the open when they know their strength. Heavy soils can be lightened with grit, light ones can be improved by rotted manure, or compost, or peat and general fertilizer. On the whole it makes life easier if you stick to growing those things which your particular soil grows best. If finding out what kind of soil you have seems elaborate, ask a local who is a keen gardener to get a rough idea of what does well, and look it up in the index to see where it features. Rhododendrons are not included, because they seem to me too large or alien for mixed plantings in small gardens, but most other plants ought to be somewhere in the book. Gardening books lay down hard and fast rules about what does well where, but in real life things are often quite different. Look at the bupleurum in shade (see Chapter 9) or the

indigofera growing near a willow (see Chapter 13). Some things will fail when you expect them to thrive and others will grow by leaps and bounds when their prospects seemed gloomy. There will be disasters, there always are, but it gives you a chance to try something else. If the conditions suggested for a planting are not at all like those on offer, it would be better to try another plan, but on the whole the plants are not difficult, and if they are, substitutes are given.

STRUCTURE

Structure is what matters most in a garden, but there are different ways of providing it. A formal framework can pull together the most amorphous collection of plants: straight lines, circles, hedges, buttresses and repeated plants will all make up for a host of deficiencies in the planting. Think of walking down a grass path between borders backed by yew hedges and punctuated by some sort of shaped plant – an upright rosemary, perhaps on either side, and the odd dome of lavender. Even if the formal beds were only filled with indifferent large daisies they would still look better than an island bed which contained only those daisies, lavender and rosemary. Beds which have no structure of their own need plants to provide some shape. They need strong masses of form to hold the eye and to stop it wandering all over the place and they need a much more thought-out approach within the bed to make up for the lack of order without. This means choosing plants which have some architectural value, of which more are needed in informal settings than in formal ones. The best arrangements always include a few and this is why certain plants recur throughout the book: plants with large leaves, or spiky ones, or shrubs which make regular shapes that look like columns or domes or outspread hands. If you leave these out, everything looks rather flat and hopeless. Often the structure comes from evergreens and this is important in winter, because if no evergreens are included the bed will look deadly for five months of the year; this need not matter if your garden is large enough to provide a view, or if you can arrange to spend those months on the Riviera, but most people like to have something to cheer them up when the weather turns nasty.

Many of the plants which will dominate a planting after five years are slow to start, but it is vital to give them the room and encouragement to grow. The scale of a planting alters in an extraordinary way as it matures, which always comes as a surprise to beginners. You need to know this, so that you can adjust as the plants change in importance, and it is one of the hardest things to master of all. If, for example, you were setting out to recreate a bed from this book you would find that in the first year the herbaceous plants, like the hardy geraniums which appear in so many plans, had easily filled their allotted quarters, but that the trees or shrubs in the same border were practically stationary and about a tenth of their ultimate size. All this is very testing and you have to be patient and keep the peace between the hares and the tortoises, allowing the hares only so much space to run rings round the tortoises and remembering that the tortoise must always be allowed to win in the end.

DISTANCE

The spacing of plants, bearing in mind the hare and tortoise situation, is very tricky. The average shrub will ultimately spread to at least six feet, often more, which means that if you are planting shrubs next to one another you should allow enough room for their final girth (probably about seven feet between the two). The plans, which are drawn to scale, are of mature borders and distances between plants in their infancy will seem ludicrous. The temptation to nudge them nearer to one another will be irresistible. There will be huge gaps of brown earth where weeds will grow. Despair will set in, the planting will be pronounced impossible and the plans an inaccurate invention. Designs drawn up in a landscape architect's office are much more likely to end in failure than these, which are living proof in gardens all over the country that a particular arrangement of plants does what it is described as doing, and not what someone hoped it might do. A layout may have started life as something quite different, but it was seen and recorded, working properly, as you see it on the page.

There are several measures which can be taken to make a bed look furnished while it is in its infancy. Buying large plants can be expensive and many things establish themselves better when they are small, but it is occasionally worth splashing out on big ones if they are important to the structure. It sometimes pays to buy three of a shrub and put them in close together to make an instant mass. Later two of these plants will have to be sacrificed, because there will cease to be room for them all, but there may be other places in the garden where you could use them. On the whole, fast growing shrubs (and the catalogues will tell you which these are) tend not to move as well as slow growing ones. Ceanothus and buddleia grow so quickly it is hardly worth faking a more solid appearance by buying three, and you would have to throw the extra ones away because they hate being transplanted. Box and yew are inordinately slow, but delightfully easy to move, so buying extra plants would not be a waste of money. Economies can always be made with herbaceous plants which multiply rapidly, but even this can be a false move because what you save on plants you spend on the effort of weeding before the plants fill out. Closely planted ground needs much less maintaining than beds where the spacing is generous. Another technique for making borders look fuller than they are is to use annuals. The giant nicotiana (*N. sylvestris*) comes easily from seed and will make six feet in a season. Cosmos, cleome, sweet peas on sticks, or the climbing canary creeper (*Tropaeolum canariense*) and even dahlias, are all possibilities for adding height to a bed, but perhaps not all at once. Some people use quick growing temporary shrubs such as broom or buddleia among the slower growing permanent shrubs, but this can end in trouble as the understudies tend to swamp the leads.

As things grow, you may decide that you dislike what you see and feel brave enough to alter one or two plants to make it feel more like your own work. Changing and eliminating is all part of gardening and I have indicated in several places where substitutes might be made to produce quite a different emphasis. In writing the book, I learnt more about combining plants than in twenty years of looking at gardens, because instead of wandering vaguely through lovely places, enjoying a general feeling of well-being and admiring individual plants, I was really examining each one in relation to another, or as part of a whole, seeing why certain sorts of plant worked (or failed to work) and thinking about what else might have fitted the bill. Many of the gardeners who spared valuable time to help with the book denied that they ever thought about the design at all. For instinctive gardeners it is probably not so important, but for those who do not feel at ease with plants I think it helps to rationalize what seems to be a thoroughly unpredictable affair. Gardens are never quite what you expect and if you don't know what to expect anyway, no wonder you flounder. Adopting the proven experiments of experienced gardeners is a short cut, which ought to go some way towards helping you in the direction of finding your own.

CHOICE

The photographs and written descriptions are there to help you choose the sort of effect that you would like to imitate. There are strong colours and pale colours, traditional arrangements and more modern ones. Some borders are not for the uninitiated; these are the ones full of rare and almost unobtainable plants. Some are so simple that a child could plant them. I do not think that any of them bears any resemblance to the sort of instant borders sold by a few nurserymen as a package. They are all highly individual and many of them have taken years to reach the state in which you see them. There is no guarantee that your bed will end up looking exactly like the picture, any more than an oil painting by numbers will turn out to be an old master, but it ought to take on a vitality of its own as your gardening knowledge increases at the same pace as the plants in the border.

Fashions are changing in gardening as they do all the time in other art forms. People will continue to look back with nostalgia at the Sissinghurst style which has dominated our best gardens for so long, perhaps because it suits English skies and countrysides, but there are those who feel that this influence is a bad and irrelevant one. This selection errs on the side of the traditional, but there are some modern plantings including, in particular, examples of what I think is the most interesting development in twentieth-century gardening. This is not the mixed border, or the seasonal border, which do appear in the book,

but the 'mingled' or layered border. This, I think, is the one to watch. As gardens get smaller, effects need to be concentrated in one place. Texture and form, and the solid, unchanging colours of shrubs and trees are not enough for everyone. People continue to cling stubbornly to the idea of flowers. They want to see a display of flowers which is continuous, but alters with the seasons. If I had to recommend one bed from the book that does just this it would be the planting by the Chief Gardens Adviser to The National Trust (Chapter 25). Christopher Lloyd partly uses the same technique, but less florally and on a much grander scale.

Appearance is not the only criterion. It is important to know how you want to look at the border. Is it to be a place where you linger or is it a flowerbed which is most often seen in the distance? From the windows of the house a bed must look good in winter as well as summer; if it is out of sight you can concentrate on making a show for the months when you can be outdoors. Double borders, with a path between, are always effective; there are plenty of them in this book but most are best seen by walking down their length rather than viewing them head on. This is also true for single borders. On all the plans north has been indicated, though the bed does not need to face the same direction in your garden, but if it falls in total shade, it would be unwise to choose a full sun design, and vice versa. Beds which face west are generally warmer than those which face east, but the amount of sunshine received can be affected by neighbouring trees, so take these into account. In winter, because of the angle of the sun, the shading from trees is much greater than it is in high summer and there may appear to be no part of the garden where you can site a sunny border, so decisions ought to be delayed until you are certain of where the sun shines all year round. Plant hardiness can vary within a few square miles, but as a general rule the most favoured gardens are those where drainage is good, the climate is warm and there is shelter from winds. In cold places things can be grown in light soil (sandy or gravelly) out of the wind that might fail in warmer climates on heavy clay, so it is not just the question of climate which restricts what you can grow.

HOW TO USE THE BOOK

Each border has a scaled plan drawn with infinite care by Gemma Nesbitt, who, although not a gardener herself, has brought an artist's and an amateur's eye to the problem of making diagrams intelligible to ordinary people. So often garden plans are drawn like overlapping scales, which means that you cannot see where one thing ends and another begins. It is true that plants flow into one another as they grow, but when they are planted they don't, and keeping them distinct, as they are here, should help people to see what ought to go where. Designer's plans very often have numbers instead of names which refer you to a list, so that you bob back and forward and never quite remember what you are looking at. These plans have names, and

very often English names, so that you can quickly spot the more common plants like honeysuckle, or foxgloves, or the odd clump of yew, helping those who are unfamiliar with botanical names. Identifying the plants was very taxing, for many of the things were out of flower when we went back to make the plans, sometimes with the rain pouring onto the paper as Gemma drew and I dictated, but every single one has been checked with the help of the owners and all should now be correct and in place. The important plants tend to have stronger outlines than those which matter less, and the plants which seed themselves, or are underplanted like bulbs, or added like annuals, are sometimes shown only on the lists. The overriding aim was that the plans should be clear and not muddle the onlooker with too much information and that they should give some feeling of the shape and balance of the borders.

If the drawings do not tempt people into gardening who have never bought a pair of wellington boots, I cannot imagine what will. The lists contain the proper names of plants as well as their more familiar ones. The numbers given for each plant are the quantity I would consider necessary to achieve some sort of effect in two or three years. The impatient could double or, occasionally in large borders, treble the order; the impoverished could halve some of the quantities of herbaceous plants, but as most of these numbers are quite restrained it would be better to stick to those suggested. I have cut down on things which grow very quickly and I think the lists, on the

whole, are on the economical side. As a rule, quantity of underplanting and summer bedding has not been indicated but can be selected according to taste and pocket. If more than one plant is represented in the drawings, this has been indicated where space allows.

There are very few cultivating hints but it is assumed that some general gardening books will be consulted to reduce the blind-date element. There is a reading list at the back of the book and also a list of suppliers. Many of the plants suggested will not be found in every garden centre. It does not mean that they are difficult to grow, just that they are uncommercial. It does nurseries good to be asked for unusual plants, for if nobody asks, they prune their lists even more ruthlessly than before, leaving nothing but the sort of serviceable shrubs found in public plantings. Private gardening is different: it ought to be idiosyncratic and selective. If you can be bothered to shop around for unusual things for the house, or for delicious things to eat, why not apply the same standards out of doors? It is very hard for the dedicated gardener to see what prevents people, who are otherwise infinitely civilized, from realizing that gardening represents an art form, and is not just a chance to show off horticultural skills. I hope this book will help to tip the balance away from horticulture and towards the fine and civilized pursuit of making a garden.

1

MONET COLOURS IN A COBBLED HERB GARDEN

A cobbled garden planted with a mixture of herbs, vegetables and flowers is in a very English tradition. This is the way things were done at Sissinghurst where, within the austerity of Harold Nicolson's straight lines, Vita Sackville-West indulged in the rich planting and romantic profusion which occurs in the best cottage gardens. Before Sissinghurst existed, William Robinson, the Victorian advocate of the wild garden, had pronounced that formality is essential to the plan of a garden, but never to the arrangement of its flowers and shrubs. Gertrude Jekyll, who worked with Lutyens, was another admirer of this style of planting which has lasted for centuries, continuing all over the land in walled gardens and around cottages, even during the time when the eighteenth-century English landscape movement was at its height.

Random placing of plants – the odd courgette surrounded by flowers – looks positively deliberate if the framework of the design is as strong as it is here. Hedges of beech and box and lines of espaliered fruit surround the plot. The variety of apple chosen is 'Wagener', which is an American spring dessert apple, a good cropper and easy to grow, but the choice was perhaps influenced by childhood memories of one of the garden's owners, for he is American by birth. 'Tydeman's Late Orange' or 'Orleans Reinette' would be possible alternatives if a more familiar apple was preferred. In the centre of the garden clumps of silver lamb's ear and the purple bugle, which has blue flowers, line both sides of the path. Eight bushes of artemisia (southernwood) are ranged behind this edging and all this leads up to an arch covered in the rose 'Goldfinch'. In each of the four central beds the pattern of planting is roughly the same, with a large plant (a peony or a courgette) in the middle, surrounded by a muddle of flowers. It is interesting to see that there are four artemisias in one of the beds, a

relic of an earlier and even more formal treatment, but this was abandoned because it did not leave enough room for a variety of plants. Less adventurous gardeners might like to copy the discarded formal plan, repeating it either in the bed opposite on the other side of the path, or even in all four beds. There would still be some space for a certain amount of other flowers, but the general effect would be much more orderly and would involve less work.

In these central beds purple and blue predominate, backed up by silver, yellow, pink and white, but at the edge of the garden bright blues and oranges from marigolds and felicia, against the deep blues of delphiniums, look like patches of Monet's garden where 'Colour is all'. Colour is currently a low priority with gardeners who prefer to concentrate on texture and shape and who fight shy of

OPPOSITE: *Orange and blue flowers are an antidote to the vogue for 'white' gardens.*

14

anything more daring than white. Such discretion is dull and these beds designed by a painter and his wife ought to be an inspiration to others to plan gardens where colour is just as important as structure.

The White Garden at Sissinghurst has influenced many gardeners to plant pale imitations of that wonderfully luminous place, but what most people choose to ignore at Sissinghurst is the use of colour. The purple border in the courtyard, the sunset oranges of the cottage garden and the rich crimsons of the old roses all illustrate a riot of colour, something that is generally despised by people of taste, who favour pastel shades with touches of silver. In John Hubbard's planting the balance of colour is a joy. It takes a painter to get it absolutely right and even if the colour scheme chosen here is not adopted, it would be possible to replace it with another, provided the distribution of colours remained the same, but it would be difficult and it would take someone with a very good eye to achieve anything as pretty.

In late summer the salvias are the mainstay of the beds, but some of the varieties chosen are not hardy. *Salvia involucrata* 'Bethelli' is a lovely thing, which is better grown by owners of greenhouses, because although it can survive out of doors in cooler places than southern England, it takes a whole summer

OPPOSITE: *Romantic profusion is in the best Sissinghurst tradition. Here vertical plants such as foxgloves and lilies rise above low mounds of herbs. The odd accident like the orange poppy is allowed to stay.*

to grow to flowering stature and is only just beginning to come into its own when the first frosts start. *Salvia neurepia* is tricky too, but grows quickly from cuttings which can spend the winter on a windowsill. Other delicate plants are *Geranium maderense* and the penstemons (although 'Garnet') should survive. Some of the richness of the planting would obviously be lost if substitutes were used, but possible alternatives might be *Monarda didyma* 'Cambridge Scarlet' instead of the salvias, *Geranium psilostemon* for *G. maderense* and ordinary crimson snapdragons as a replacement for the penstemons. The little blue daisy, *Felicia amelloides*, can disappear over a winter so *Aster thomsonii* would be more reliable and would flower for almost as long, but it is not such a clear blue nor so graceful as the felicia. None of these things would be as distinguished as the plants chosen, but they would be serviceable and easy and would give some of the flavour of the original. It is the attention to detail, the choosing of the best forms of plants that puts a garden into a different class. Here the true French tarragon (*Artemisia dracunculus sativa*) is preferred to the Russian form, which often masquerades as the French, and the purple version of basil is grown. This is as delicious as it is decorative, but its constitution seems less strong than the usual variety. Some plants which are easy, but not often seen, are the airy *Gillenia trifoliata* and the pyramidal ajuga, which grows wild on the rocks of northern Scotland. Like this ajuga, other plants in the garden – artemisia, stachys and foxgloves – can be grown in poor soil, but

the majority like a well-drained place in the sun with plenty of humus and, for the sake of the lilies, penstemons, courgettes and annuals grown here, a fertile bed is provided. This is the sort of gardening that is hard work and it shows.

LIST OF PLANTS

In the beds illustrated in detail:

BED A
1 row *Anthriscus cerefolium* (chervil)
5 *Calendula officinalis* (marigold)
1 *Felicia amelloides* (blue African daisy)
1 row *Ocimum basilicum* and purple form (basil)
1 row *Salvium horminum* (clary)
1 row *Satureja hortensis* (summer savory)

BED B
6 *Ajuga pyramidalis*
7 *Allium christophii*
2 *Artemisia abrotanum* (southernwood, lad's love)
1 Courgette
1 *Eryngium variifolium*
1 *Geranium sanguineum lancastriense*
1 *Gypsophila paniculata* 'Rosy Veil'
9 *Lilium regale* (regale lilies)
1 *Penstemon* 'Garnet'
1 *Penstemon* 'True Blue'
3 *Salvia haematodes*
1 *Salvia involucrata* 'Bethelli'
1 *Salvia nemorosa superba* 'Lubeca'
1 *Salvia transcaucasica* (possible substitute *Salvia turkestanica*)
6 *Stachys lanata* (lamb's ear)

In the beds not illustrated in detail:

BED C (quantities to taste)
Allium schoenoprasum (chives)
Artemisia dracunculus sativa (French tarragon)
Borago officinalis (borage)
Chrysanthemum parthenium (feverfew)
Felicia amelloides
Mentha × *gentilis* 'Variegata' (Scotch mint)

17

Detail of Bed A and Bed B

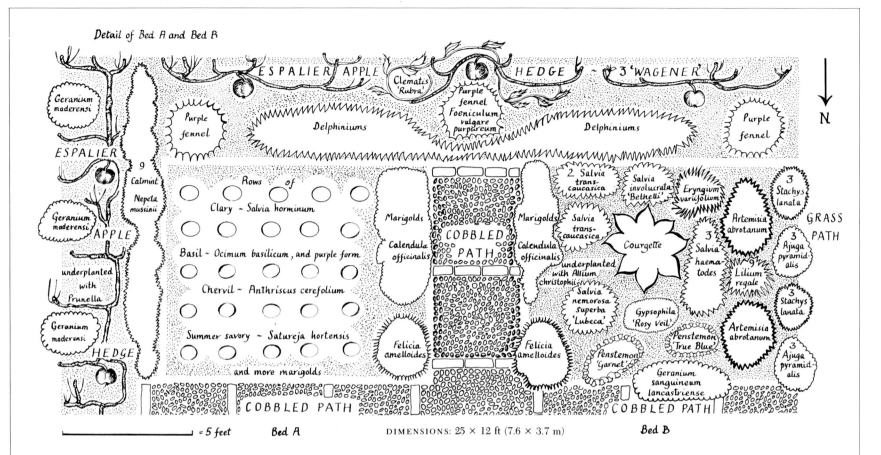

DIMENSIONS: 25 × 12 ft (7.6 × 3.7 m)

= 5 feet Bed A Bed B

Origanum vulgare (marjoram)
Rumex acetosa (sorrel)
Ruta graveolens 'Jackman's Blue' (rue)
Salvia farinacea 'Blue Bedder'
Salvia officinalis (culinary sage)
Salvia officinalis 'Icterina' (golden sage)
Salvia officinalis 'Tricolor' (sage)
Salvia patens
Tanacetum vulgare (tansy)
Thymus vulgaris (thyme)

BED D (quantities to taste)
Ajuga reptans 'Atropurpurea'
Allium moly
Artemisia arbrotanum

Artemisia canescens
Artemisia 'Lambrook Silver'
Cistus 'Silver Pink'
Felicia amelloides
Gillenia trifoliata
Gladiolus 'The Bride'
Hosta fortunei 'Albopicta'
Lilium regale
Limonium latifolium 'Violetta' (sea lavender, statice)
Meconopsis cambrica (Welsh poppy)
Paeonia 'Duchesse de Nemours'
Salvia haematodes
Salvia neurepia
Salvia × superba 'Lubeca'

Stachys lanata (lamb's ear)
Verbena rigida
Viola × wittrockiana (pansy): 'Ullswater' (blue); 'Sunny Boy' (yellow)

BED E (quantities to taste)
Allium moly
Artemisia arbrotanum
Courgette
Chrysanthemum 'Mawri'
Geranium psilostemon
Lilium regale
Penstemon 'Sour Grapes'
Salvia involucrata 'Bethelli'
Thalictrum aquilegifolium

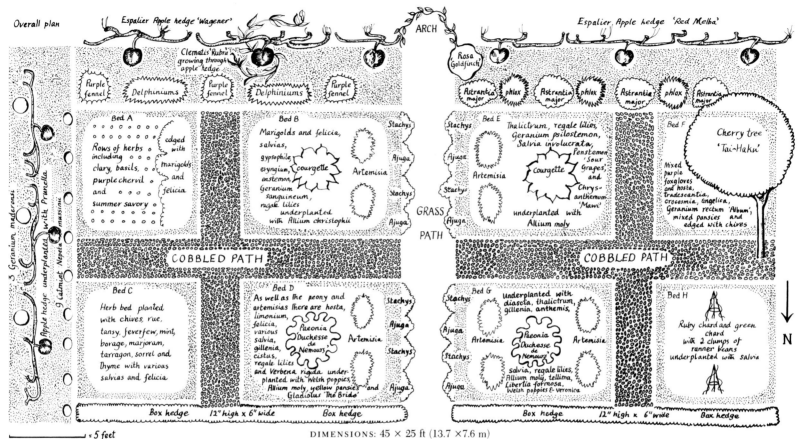

Overall plan

Espalier Apple hedge 'Wagener'   ARCH   Espalier Apple hedge 'Red Melba'

Clematis 'Rubra' growing through apple hedge

Rosa Goldfinch

Purple fennel — Delphiniums — Purple fennel — Delphiniums — Purple fennel

Astrantia major · phlox · Astrantia major · phlox · Astrantia major · phlox · Astrantia major

3 Geranium maderense
Apple hedge underplanted with Prunella
9 catmint Nepeta musinii

Bed A
Rows of herbs including clary, basils, purple chervil and summer savory
edged with marigolds and felicia

Bed B
Marigolds and felicia, salvias, gypsophile, eryngium, enstemon, Geranium sanguineum, regale lilies underplanted with Allium christophii
courgette
Stachys · Ajuga · Artemisia · Stachys · Ajuga

Bed E
Stachys · Ajuga · Artemisia · Stachys · Ajuga
Thalictrum, regale lilies, Geranium psilostemon, Salvia involucrata, Penstemon 'Sour Grapes', and Chrysanthemum 'Mawi'
Courgette
underplanted with Allium moly

GRASS PATH

Bed F
Cherry tree 'Tai-Haku'
Mixed purple foxgloves and hosta, tradescantia, angelica, crocosmia, Geranium rectum 'Album', mixed pansies and edged with chives

COBBLED PATH   COBBLED PATH

Bed C
Herb bed planted with chives, rue, tansy, feverfew, mint, borage, marjoram, tarragon, sorrel and thyme with various salvias and felicia

Bed D
As well as the peony and artemisias there are hosta, limonium, felicia, various salvia, gillenia, cistus, regale lilies and Verbena rigida underplanted with Welsh poppies, Allium moly, yellow pansies and Gladiolus 'The Bride'
Paeonia 'Duchesse de Nemours'
Stachys · Ajuga · Artemisia · Stachys · Ajuga

Bed G
Stachys · Ajuga · Artemisia · Stachys · Ajuga
Underplanted with diascia, thalictrum, gillenia, anthemis,
Paeonia Duchesse de Nemours
salvia, regale lilies, Allium moly, tellima, Libertia formosa, Welsh poppies & veronica.

Bed H
Ruby chard and green chard with 2 clumps of runner beans underplanted with salvia

N

Box hedge   12" high × 6" wide   Box hedge
Box hedge   12" high × 6" wide   Box hedge

= 5 feet   DIMENSIONS: 45 × 25 ft (13.7 ×7.6 m)

BED F (quantities to taste)
Angelica archangelica
Crocosmia masonorum
Digitalis purpurea (mixed foxgloves)
Geranium rectum 'Album'
Hosta albomarginata
Prunus 'Tai-haku' (cherry tree)
Tradescantia virginiana

BED G (quantities to taste)
Ajuga reptans 'Atropurpurea'
Allium moly
Anthemis cupaniana
Artemisia arbrotanum

Artemisia 'Lambrook Silver'
Artemisia stelleriana 'Boughton'
Lilium regale
Meconopsis cambrica (Welsh poppy)
Paeonia 'Duchesse de Nemours'
Rehmannia guttata (or *Digitalis* 'Foxy')
Salvia grahamii
Salvia leucantha (or *Diascia rigescens*)
Stachys lanata
Tellima grandiflora

BED H (quantities to taste)
Green chard; ruby chard; runner beans; *Salvia horminum*

SURROUNDING THE GARDEN
4 *Astrantia major*
36 *Buxus sempervirens* 'Suffruticosa' (dwarf box)
1 *Clematis viticella* 'Rubra'
6 *Delphinium* 'Pacific Hybrid'
3 Espalier Apple 'Red Melba'
6 Espalier Apple 'Wagener'
3 *Foeniculum vulgare purpureum* (purple fennel)
3 *Geranium maderense*
9 *Nepeta musinii* (catmint)
3 *Phlox paniculata* 'Hampton Court'
1 *Prunus* 'Tai-haku' (cherry tree)
1 *Rosa* 'Goldfinch'

2

A Bold Design for a Low Maintenance Border

This is a smart border. Glossy and effective at a distance, it is designed to be seen from the terrace and the windows of the house and to make an impact for most of the year. Peter Coats designs borders which are easy to look after and which rely on foliage for most of their colour. Gold, purple and pink predominate here and there is plenty of evergreen for winter. At the back of the bed five buttresses of pyracantha were originally planned against the red brick wall, which is topped by a white trellis fence, but these have been allowed to grow into loose shrubs and now interfere with the architectural lines. It might have been better to subdue them into more formal shapes, as was originally intended. On the other hand, if they do go on growing until they join, the border will then be set off against a background of evergreen. Pyracantha makes a good backcloth for any planting: it grows quickly and is evergreen in winter; it has white hawthorn flowers in summer and scarlet ber-

ries late in the year and there is a case for seeing as much of it as possible.

Gardening is as much about making choices over how to grow something as it is about what to grow and where to put it. Plants can look quite different grown formally and can set the scene just by the way they are shaped and placed, so deciding how to treat them is important if you want to achieve a consistent style. One of the questions to think about when planning a border is whether it is to look ordered, with bold defined clumps of plants, or whether to go for a looser flowing style where the plants drift into each other in a more natural-looking way. In plantings which rely on shrubs the overall effect tends to be harder, but perennials like the cranesbills which have been used here can help to blur the edges.

The contrast of colour is strong. Bright acid yellow of *Robinia* 'Frisia' and gold of lonicera and the 'Goldflame' spiraea show up against the purple of the cotinus and the bronzy crim-

son leaves of the acer. All these shrubs grow fast and it would be vital to keep them in their places by some hard pruning if the border was not to become dominated by their loud patches of colour. In any border where shrubs and perennials are combined, keeping the balance between the plants which grow strongly and those which dwindle and fade is always important. This border would become dull and rather municipal if the smaller things were eased out, but if the strong background is kept in order it will show off and define the other plants.

Peonies are good plants to use in bold borders. Some of them, as well as the tree peony, were already in the garden when the border was made. There are other strong herbaceous plants which might be included in a similar arrangement: acanthus, morina, or

OPPOSITE: *An easy-to-maintain bed which relies on strong groups of bold colours below a decorative fence.*

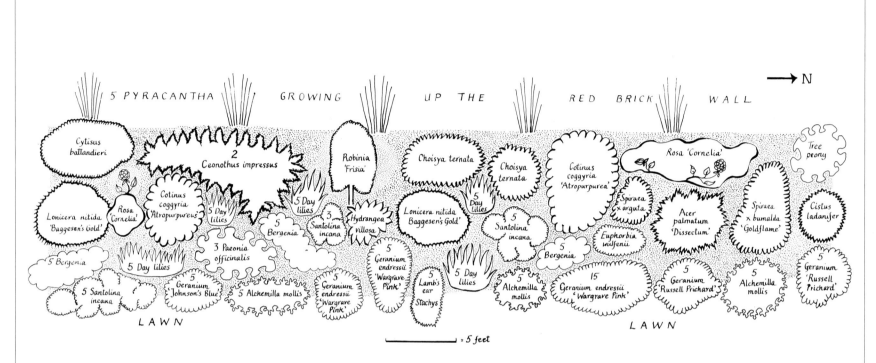

Cytisus battandieri

2 Ceonothus impressus

Robinia 'Frisia'

Choisya ternata

Choisya ternata

Cotinus coggyria 'Atropurpurea'

Rosa 'Cornelia'

Tree peony

Lonicera nitida 'Baggesen's Gold'

Rosa 'Cornelia'

Cotinus coggyria 'Atropurpureus'

5 Day lilies

5 Day lilies

3 Santolina incana

Hydrangea villosa

Lonicera nitida 'Baggesen's Gold'

5 Day lilies

Santolina incana

Spiraea × arguta

Acer palmatum 'Dissectum'

Spiraea × bumalda 'Goldflame'

Cistus ladanifer

5 Bergenia

Bergenia

Euphorbia wulfenii

Bergenia

5 Bergenia

5 Day lilies

3 Paeonia officinalis

Geranium endressii 'Wargrave Pink'

5 Lamb's ear Stachys

5 Day lilies

5 Alchemilla mollis

15 Geranium endressii 'Wargrave Pink'

5 Geranium 'Russell Prichard'

5 Alchemilla mollis

5 Geranium 'Russell Prichard'

5 Santolina incana

5 Day lilies

Geranium 'Johnson's Blue'

5 Alchemilla mollis

5 Geranium endressii 'Wargrave Pink'

LAWN

LAWN

= 5 feet

DIMENSIONS: 54 × 12 ft (16.5 × 3.7 m)

hellebores and any of the hosta tribe would all be able to hold their own. Small treasures are probably best left out of large scale effects like this unless they can be planted in masses, and anything which needs cosseting would also be best ignored.

LIST OF PLANTS

 1 *Acer palmatum* 'Dissectum'
15 *Alchemilla mollis*
15 *Bergenia* 'Ballawley'
 2 *Ceanothus impressus*

 2 *Choisya ternata*
 1 *Cistus ladanifer*
 1 *Cotinus coggyria* 'Foliis Purpureis'
 1 *Cytisus battandieri*
 1 *Euphorbia wulfenii*
25 *Geranium endressii* 'Wargrave Pink'
 5 *Geranium* 'Johnson's Blue'
10 *Geranium* 'Russell Prichard'
25 *Hemerocallis* (day lilies)
 1 *Hydrangea villosa*
 2 *Lonicera nitida* 'Baggesen's Gold'
 3 *Paeonia officinalis*
 5 *Pyracantha* 'Orange Glow'
 1 *Robinia* 'Frisia'

 2 *Rosa* 'Cornelia' (musk rose hybrid)
13 *Santolina incana*
 1 *Spiraea* × *arguta*
 1 *Spiraea* × *bumalda* 'Goldflame'
 5 *Stachys lanata* (lamb's ear)
 1 *Paeonia suffruticosa* (tree peony, possible choice 'Renkaku' white)

OPPOSITE: *Peonies and blue cranesbills in a high-summer riot against the more permanent feature of silvery santolina.*

3

A WARM WALL IN A COLD CLIMATE

Dream houses are always pictured with roses round the door and a riot of growing things, which can be difficult to achieve in a stark climate. This northern garden has a look of the warm south, but to keep it this way involves careful planning. Some of the plants chosen would not survive cold winters; to grow them in Northumberland demands dedication. *Convolvulus cneorum*, the lovely silver shrub with flowers like bindweed, is difficult except in very well-drained sunny places and it often needs replacing. The purple sage, penstemons, the curry plant and silver *Chrysanthemum haradjanii* are none of them reliable and cuttings would need to be taken of all these plants every autumn. Reserve plants could then be grown in the greenhouse for putting out in the spring.

If nothing but roses and wisteria are grown on a house there will be a lot of unfurnished stems in winter. Very beautifully trained branches can provide something to look at when the leaves and flowers have gone, but a tangle of carelessly pruned summer climbers is a depressing sight in December. If pruning is a weakness, it might be better to substitute an evergreen for one of the roses. The hardier ceanothuses like 'Delight' or *C. thyrsiflorus* might do, or alternatively a not too rampant ivy grown in partnership with a rose would look green in winter. The border is a delight in summer, but in the long northern winter, with only a juniper and a few hellebores for company, the days might drag a little.

Compare this planting with the one round the shady back door in the south of England (Chapter 9) and the border on the house wall in a high, cold garden (Chapter 11), both of which include a measure of plants for the colder months. It is tempting to go overboard for a summer effect and the success of this selection shows just how tempting, but it is important to remember winter before devoting all of the available space to summer flowers. Where the planting is close to the house, and particularly where it surrounds a door which is used every day, facing the question of summer versus winter is a priority. If some of the roses had to go to make room for other plants, 'Zéphirine Drouhin' would have to stay. The thornless rose is much the best choice for flopping around a door, because then there is no danger of getting scratched, but its cerise pink is hard to combine with the coral pink of the 'Aloha' rose and the latter might be the one to take away. It would be sad to lose 'Mme Alfred Carrière', but she is very rampant and does not demand a south wall, so might be another candidate for removal. It would then be possible to include a winter jasmine with a clematis growing through in place of 'Mme Alfred Carrière' and perhaps a

OPPOSITE: *Rose-covered windows in June are dominated by the thornless pink, 'Zéphirine Drouhin'.*

daphne or a winter flowering honeysuckle in place of 'Aloha'. More lilies might be included to make up for losing the roses, so that there were still plenty of flowers in summer and it never does any harm to increase stocks of Japanese anemones. These obliging plants do not seem to mind where they grow and could be fitted in at the foot of the wall under the climbing shrubs. Aconites are a possibility below the roses (as long as there is not too much manure) to provide colour in early February. They like to be shaded in summer so would need to be planted right under the roses whose leaves will cover the flowers in the hot months. The border is lovely to look at as it stands, but a few winter underpinnings would keep it looking lovely all through the year.

RIGHT: *Clematis 'Jackmanii' is a dependable favourite which gives strong colour late in the year.*

26

LIST OF PLANTS

3 *Alchemilla mollis*
5 *Anemone hupehensis japonica* 'Honorine Jobert'
    (white Japanese anemone)
1 *Artemisia* 'Margery Fish'
1 *Chrysanthemum haradjani*
1 *Clematis* 'Jackmanii Superba'
1 *Convolvulus cneorum*
3 *Dianthus* 'White Ladies'
1 *Helianthemum* 'The Bride'
1 *Helichrysum angustifolium* (curry plant)
1 *Helleborus corsicus*
1 *Helleborus lividus* 'Boughton Beauty'
5 *Iris pallida* 'Jane Phillips'
1 *Juniperus sabina tamariscifolia*
1 *Lavandula spica* 'Hidcote' (lavender)
3 *Lilium regale* (regale lilies)
3 *Lilium speciosum* 'Rubrum'
2 *Penstemon* 'Garnet'
3 *Prunella webbiana* 'Alba'
1 *Rosa* 'Aloha'
1 *Rosa* 'Anna Louisa'
1 *Rosa* 'Apricot Silk'
1 *Rosa* 'Cardinal Richelieu'
1 *Rosa* 'Claire Jacquier'
1 *Rosa* 'Mme Alfred Carrière'
2 *Rosa* 'Penelope'
1 *Rosa* 'Zéphirine Drouhin'
2 *Salvia officinalis* 'Purpurascens' (purple sage)
1–3 *Senecio cineraria*
3 *Sisyrinchium striatum*
3 *Tradescantia andersoniana* 'J.C. Weguelin'
1 *Verbascum olympicum* (mullein)
1 *Wisteria sinensis*

DIMENSIONS: 13¼ ft long × 12 ft deep (4.1 × 3.7 m)

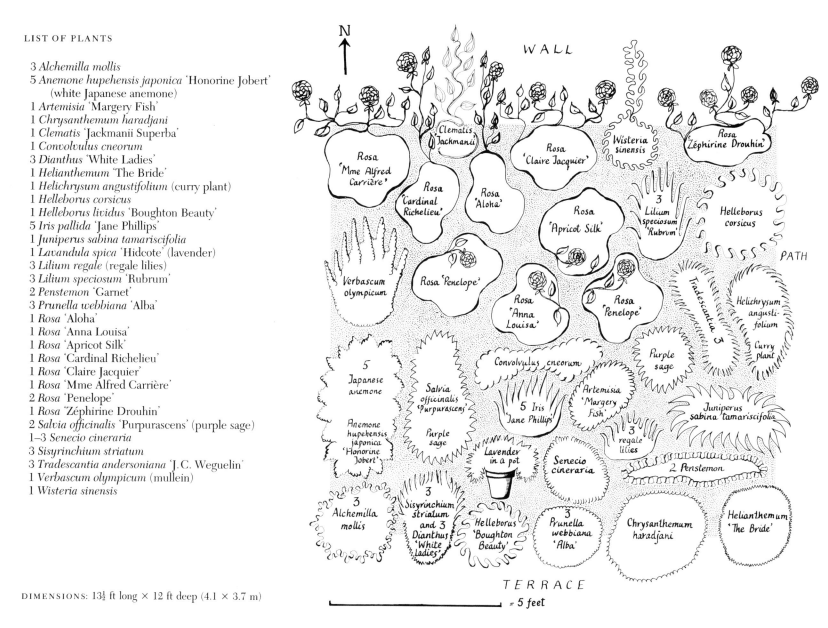

27

4

AN ARCHITECT'S WATER GARDEN

———————

Few people can resist the idea of water in a garden, but it is rare to see a pool with proportions and setting as perfect as this. The owner, a distinguished architect himself, claims that Edwin Lutyens, who was an old family friend, scribbled the design on the back of an envelope. In London, gardens which are at their peak in May tend to trail off after the roses are over and look tired and dusty, so this is a cool solution to the problem of what to look at in a garden that is past its midsummer best. It would also be a way of treating a space for those who dislike gardening; maintenance is minimal and there is not even very much mowing to do. The pool is perhaps on the large side for many people, but what matters is the relationship of the water to its surroundings, and it would be perfectly possible to scale the whole thing down. Reducing the measurements of the pool and the stone edging by half would leave three feet of grass running up to the low wall which surrounds the garden, and

any planting could then be reserved for the area above the wall.

Originally the garden had flower borders running on either side behind and above this wall, but the east-facing border has been grassed over, leaving only a line of roses and clematis trained to wires on posts to provide height at the back of where the bed would have ended. On the west side, a planting of easy midsummer flowers in rich colours flanks a seat set in the middle which looks through an archway between the roses to a view of strong foliage beyond. Behind the seat *Macleaya cordata*, the least invasive of the plume poppies, grows and in the beds are a mixture of tree peonies, fuchsias, campanulas, hemerocallis, roses, blue herbaceous veronicas and clematis. The effect is pretty and rather Edwardian in an opulent way and this border, the one opposite and a ferns and valerian border at the far end all contain the garden, providing a foil to the water at its heart.

Planting in the pool itself is restricted to only two species, waterlilies and irises, with each species represented by two varieties. More plants would only confuse the eye, and such restraint makes the pool a calm place in the middle of its flowery surround, so it is important to keep this distinction. In the chosen planting, the smaller clump in the centre of the pool is *Iris laevigata* 'Alba', which likes to have its feet in water, and the clumps on the outside are *Iris kaempferi*. These like moisture in summer, but not to be waterlogged in winter and also need lime-free soil. Easier alternatives might be *Iris sibirica* in a white or blue form, or, for large pools, the taller yellow flag *Iris pseudacorus* always looks handsome and has ornamental seed pods after

OPPOSITE: *Waterlilies surrounded by dry sun-loving plants in a formal setting. Clumps of irises by the water echo the sisyrinchium round the edge of the bed.*

Pots of sempervivums on the paving stones make people careful about where they put their feet.

both good, white, scented lilies for medium-sized pools. Waterlilies can turn into a heaving mass of leaves if they are too vigorous; the present varieties have to have pieces chopped off them annually. A small pink fragrant lily for a scaled-down pool might be N. *caroliniana*. Alternatively, smell could be sacrificed to a lengthy flowering season, in which case the rosy spotted N. × 'Laydekeri purpurata', which has flowers all summer, would be a good choice. N. *rose nymphe* is only slightly less abundant and does have the advantage of scent. 'Sunrise' is probably the most dependable of the yellows.

Around the pool grow dry-loving plants. Pinks and the small blue sisyrinchium, blue flax and mulleins, as well as the rather invasive, but pretty, white *Sedum album* all seed themselves in the best possible places. 'God's work' is how the owner refers to the starry haze growing so haphazardly out of the paving stones. The pots containing a collection of sempervivums have, however, been placed there by man for a good reason: apparently if there are pots on the ground, people look carefully at where they are going and avoid treading on the plants that are not in pots. The rather random placing of these pots and the rock plants looks better than a formal arrangement around the water's edge. The combination of strict architectural formality with the loose planting of 'God's work', and the contrast of the smooth water with the rounded lily leaves against the hazy flowers around the pool makes an unusually pretty and easy type of garden.

the flowers. It might be worth considering changing these irises round so that the taller form occupied the central position, with a lower variety on the outside. Bear in mind that whatever is planted on the island is likely to be in a moist place, whereas those at the edges could be kept dryer.

The pink and yellow waterlilies are kept in the pond for sentimental reasons and could be replaced by even better forms. In small gardens, or where plants are restricted to only a few varieties, it is always important to insist on the best. It seems a pity not to choose scented lilies in preference to others, and some people might prefer white to coloured lilies. *Nymphaea lactea* and N. *caroliniana nivea* are

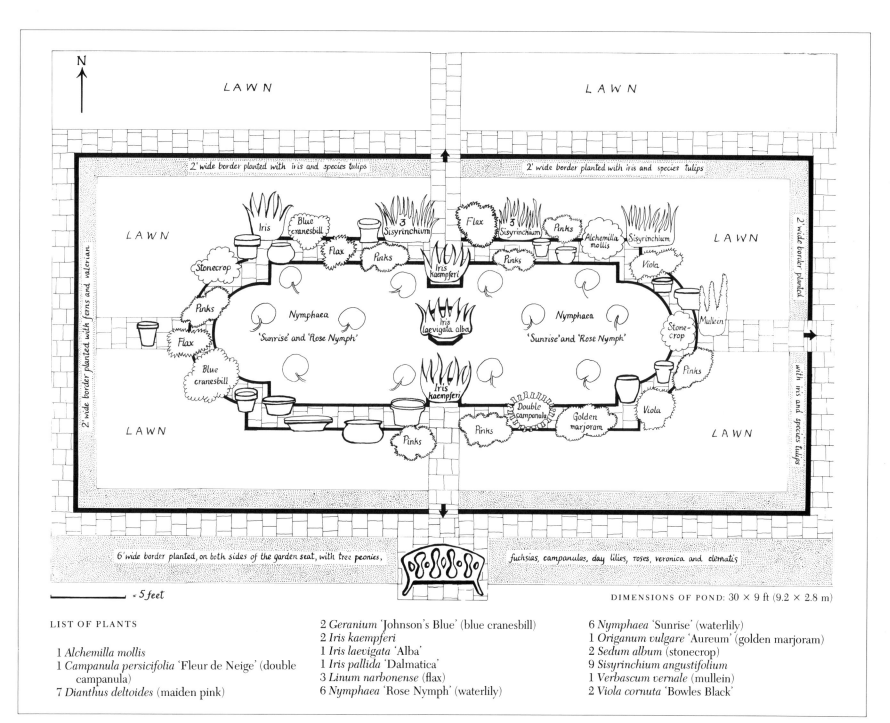

N

LAWN   LAWN

2' wide border planted with iris and species tulips   2' wide border planted with iris and species tulips

LAWN   LAWN

Iris   Blue cranesbill   3 Sisyrinchium   Flax   3 Sisyrinchium   Pinks   Alchemilla mollis   Sisyrinchium

Stonecrop   Flax   Pinks   Iris kaempferi   Pinks   Viola

Pinks   Mullein

Flax   Nymphaea 'Sunrise' and 'Rose Nymph'   Iris laevigata alba   Nymphaea 'Sunrise' and 'Rose Nymph'   Stone-crop

Blue cranesbill   Pinks

Iris kaempferi   Viola

Double campanula   Golden marjoram

Pinks   Pinks   Pinks

LAWN   LAWN

6' wide border planted, on both sides of the garden seat, with tree peonies,   fuchsias, campanulas, day lilies, roses, veronica and clematis

= 5 feet   DIMENSIONS OF POND: 30 × 9 ft (9.2 × 2.8 m)

LIST OF PLANTS

1 Alchemilla mollis

1 Campanula persicifolia 'Fleur de Neige' (double campanula)

7 Dianthus deltoides (maiden pink)

2 Geranium 'Johnson's Blue' (blue cranesbill)

2 Iris kaempferi

1 Iris laevigata 'Alba'

1 Iris pallida 'Dalmatica'

3 Linum narbonense (flax)

6 Nymphaea 'Rose Nymph' (waterlily)

6 Nymphaea 'Sunrise' (waterlily)

1 Origanum vulgare 'Aureum' (golden marjoram)

2 Sedum album (stonecrop)

9 Sisyrinchium angustifolium

1 Verbascum vernale (mullein)

2 Viola cornuta 'Bowles Black'

5

HERBS IN AUGUST

August is never an easy month in the garden, but this is the time when herbs come into their own. They are difficult plants to place because some of them are tall with insignificant flowers, while others sprawl and outgrow the boundaries of the conventional herb garden bed. Here the larger plants, which might upset the symmetry, have been mixed in with ordinary shrubs and perennials, leaving the smaller varieties to be confined to box-edged diamond beds. Keeping plants in neat knots demands a watchful eye: one sort can easily stray into another, and, where balance demands regular clumps, it is rare for everything to grow at the same rate. Formal gardens are not for gardeners who believe in *laissez-faire*. Rosemary Verey has a particular interest in historic gardens and this tight, trellised layout contains a collection of seventeenth-century culinary and medicinal plants in a contemporary setting. However, as one of our leading plantswomen, Mrs Verey believes that horticultural accidents often make the best gardens and the informal grouping of plants in the large bed illustrates a quite different approach. It is interesting to see two such opposite styles of planting using some of the same types of plants. The contrast in technique may not have been deliberate but it works surprisingly well.

At the back of the large bed, evergreens and spring shrubs provide something to look at early in the year. In the spring there is plenty of white from spiraea, choisya and the variegated leaves of the cornus. These are seen against a background of green because whichever way you walk down the path, there are buttresses of evergreen to edge the bed. Holly, ivy, yew and box stand at one end and at the other a huge bush of choisya provides a green focus. When a border is always viewed lengthways and rarely head on, it is a good idea to give it an important edge, like the wings of a stage, to back the planting.

A row of peonies marks the line of an earlier path. Peonies never like to be moved and any gardener who puts plants before design would always leave well alone, which is probably why they have been allowed to stay where they have always been. Domes and splashes of evergreen and gold are repeated in this bed, as they are throughout the rest of the garden. While these look lovely in a setting of Cotswold stone walls and buildings, the gold might be out of place in red-brick country. In late summer there is more gold from the flowers of fennel and from the long flowering dyer's greenweed.

There are two moments in the year when the beds are overhauled. In autumn, forget-me-nots and wallflowers, as well as plenty of bulbs, are dropped into every available space and at the start of summer there is a mad

OPPOSITE: *Yellow dyer's greenweed, fennel flowers and golden elder produce a sunny effect against the darker greens for a long season.*

rush to place plants grown from seed, which vary from year to year. White seems to be a recurring choice here: nicotianas, *Lychnis coronararia* 'Alba', *Lavatera* 'Mont Blanc' and petunias are some of the flowers which might go into the beds annually. Drifts of these white plants are taken right to the back of the border, as are other coloured annuals all over the garden. This seems to anchor the annuals to the flowerbed much more successfully than the odd spot or edge of summer bedding so often seen in other gardens.

In the formal beds, grey-leaved plants like rue and santolina are cut back hard at the end of April; the sage is done slightly later. The box is always tightly trimmed and everything else is kept in order. Thymes and sages need replacing every two or three years and the more invasive plants, such as salad burnet and variegated cress, have to be kept within bounds. Viewed from afar, the formal pattern looks like a band of trellis edging to the larger flowerbed. Even after one of the hottest summers on record, when the grass browned and most plants wilted, everything in these beds looked sunny and fresh.

LEFT: *In a hot summer when the lawn is scorched brown, groups of herbs are still presentable.*

RIGHT: *Domes and splashes of evergreen and gold look lovely in a setting of Cotswold stone walls.*

DIMENSIONS OF HERB BORDER: 38 × 5 ft (11.6 × 1.5 m), with path 3 ft (0.9 m) wide

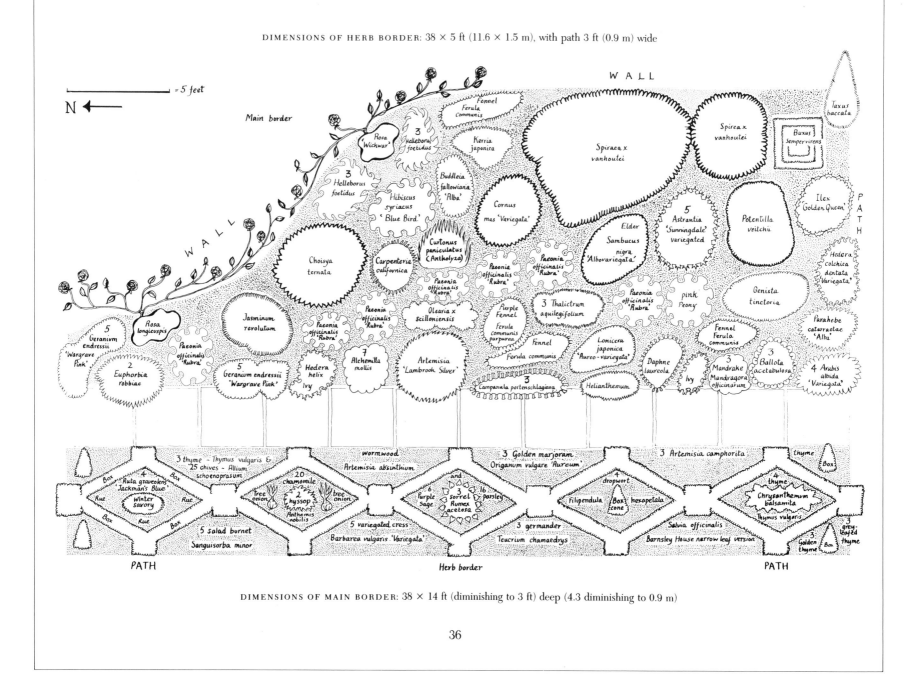

= 5 feet

N

WALL

WALL

Main border

Rosa 'Wickwar'

Helleborus foetidus

Fennel Ferula communis

Kerria japonica

Spirea x vanhoutei

Taxus baccata

Buxus Sempervirens

3 Helleborus foetidus

Hibiscus syriacus 'Blue Bird'

Buddleia fallowiana 'Alba'

Cornus mas 'Variegata'

Spiraea x vanhoutei

5 Astrantia 'Sunningdale' variegated

Potentilla veitchii

Ilex 'Golden Queen'

Choisya ternata

Carpenteria californica

Curtonus paniculatus (Antholyza)

Paeonia officinalis 'Rubra'

Paeonia officinalis 'Rubra'

Paeonia officinalis 'Rubra'

Elder Sambucus nigra 'Albovariegata'

Hedera colchica dentata 'Variegata'

Paeonia officinalis 'Rubra'

pink Peony

Genista tinctoria

5 Geranium endressii 'Wargrave Pink'

Rosa longicuspis

Jasminum revolutum

Paeonia officinalis 'Rubra'

Olearia x scilloniensis

Purple Fennel

3 Thalictrum aquilegifolium

Parahebe catarractae 'Alba'

2 Euphorbia robbiae

Paeonia officinalis 'Rubra'

Geranium endressii 'Wargrave Pink'

Hedera helix Ivy

7 Alchemilla mollis

Artemisia 'Lambrook Silver'

Ferula communis purpurea

Fennel

Ferula communis

Lonicera japonica 'Aureo-variegata'

Daphne laureola

Fennel Ferula communis

3 Mandrake Mandragora officinarum

Ivy

3 Ballota acetabulosa

4 Arabis albida 'Variegata'

Campanula portenschlagiana

Helianthemum

DIMENSIONS OF MAIN BORDER: 38 × 14 ft (diminishing to 3 ft) deep (4.3 diminishing to 0.9 m)

3 thyme - Thymus vulgaris & 25 chives - Allium schoenoprasum

wormwood Artemisia absinthium

3 Golden marjoram Origanum vulgare 'Aureum'

3 Artemisia camphorita

thyme

Box

4 Ruta graveolens Jackman's Blue

Box

Rue

Winter savory

Rue

Box

Box

20 chamomile

2 hyssop

Anthemis nobilis

tree onion

tree onion

6 purple Sage

and

3 sorrel Rumex acetosa

16 parsley

4 dropwort

Box cone

Filipendula

Box cone

R. hexapetala

4 thyme

Chrysanthemum balsamita

Thymus vulgaris

Box

5 salad burnet Sanguisorba minor

5 variegated cress Barbarea vulgaris 'Variegata'

3 germander Teucrium chamaedrys

Salvia officinalis Barnsley House narrow leaf version

3 greyleaf thyme

3 Golden thyme

Box

PATH

Herb border

PATH

36

LIST OF PLANTS

MAIN BORDER
7 *Alchemilla mollis*
4 *Arabis albida* 'Variegata'
1 *Artemisia* 'Lambrook Silver'
5 *Astrantia* 'Sunningdale'
3 *Ballota acetabulosa*
1 *Buddleia fallowiana* 'Alba'
1 *Buxus sempervirens* (box)
3 *Campanula portenschlagiana*
1 *Carpenteria californica*
1 *Choisya ternata*
1 *Cornus mas* 'Variegata'
1 *Curtonus paniculatus*
1 *Daphne laureola*
2 *Euphorbia robbiae*
3 *Ferula communis* (fennel)
1 *Ferula communis purpurea* (fennel)
1 *Genista tinctoria* (dyer's greenweed)
10 *Geranium endressi* 'Wargrave Pink'
1 *Hedera colchica* 'Dentata Variegata' (ivy)
2 *Hedera helix* 'Arborescens' (ivy)
1 *Helianthemum* 'The Bride'
6 *Helleborus foetidus*
1 *Hibiscus syriacus* 'Blue Bird'
1 *Ilex* 'Golden Queen' (holly)
1 *Jasminum revolutum*

1 *Kerria japonica*
1 *Lonicera japonica* 'Aureo-variegata'
3 *Mandragora officinarum* (mandrake)
1 *Olearia* × *scilloniensis*
1 *Paeonia* (pink, unnamed single)
7 *Paeonia officinalis* 'Rubra'
1 *Parahebe catarractae* 'Alba'
1 *Potentilla veitchii*
1 *Rosa longicuspis*
1 *Rosa* 'Wickwar' (souleana hybrid)
1 *Sambucus nigra* 'Albovariegata' (elder)
2 *Spiraea* × *vanhoutei*
1 *Taxus baccata* (yew)
3 *Thalictrum aquilegifolium*

Underplanting and summer bedding:
Allium rosenbachianum
Antirrhinums (snapdragons)
Cheiranthus cheiri (wallflowers)
Crocus speciosus
Galanthus elwesii (snowdrops)
Lavatera 'Mont Blanc' (mallow)
Lunaria annua 'Variegata' (honesty; white)
Lychnis coronaria 'Alba'
Myosotis (forget-me-not)
Nicotiana sylvestris (tobacco plant)
Petunias
Polemonium (Jacob's ladder)
Tulips

HERB BORDER
2 *Allium cepa* (tree onion)
25 *Allium schoenoprasum* (chives)
20 *Anthemis nobilis* (chamomile)
1 *Artemisia absinthium* (wormwood)
3 *Artemisia camphorita*
5 *Barbarea vulgaris* 'Variegata' (variegated cress)
5 *Buxus sempervirens* (box cone)
120 *Buxus* 'Suffruticosa' (box)
1 *Chrysanthemum balsamita*
4 *Filipendula hexapetala* (dropwort)
2 *Hyssopus officinalis* (hyssop)
3 *Origanum vulgare* 'Aureum' (golden marjoram)
16 *Petroselenum crispum* (parsley)
3 *Rumex acetosa* (sorrel)
4 *Ruta graveolens* 'Jackmans Blue' (rue)
1 *Salvia officinalis* (Barnsley House narrow leaf version)
6 *Salvia officinalis* 'Purpurascens' (purple sage)
5 *Sanguisorba minor* (salad burnet)
1 *Satureja montana* (winter savory)
3 *Teucrium chamaedrys* (germander)
3 *Thymus* × *citriodorus* 'Aureus' (golden thyme)
3 *Thymus doerfleri* (grey-leafed thyme)
7 *Thymus vulgaris* (thyme)

6

A Handsome Shrub Planting

Young shrubs and trees in pots in the local garden centre give the customer no indication of what their ultimate size and shape will be. Often in gardens one sees a shrub in an isolated lump near the front of a border, like a person at a party looking round for a companion. It is quite clear that the owner never visualized how the bush would look after five or six years, and it is also clear that it is now too late to correct the mistake. The loner will never become part of a whole picture and, as the years advance, it will stick out even more uncomfortably. In the border illustrated in this chapter, whoever planted it seems to have known where to put the fairly ordinary things that were chosen so that they would end up blending together into a satisfactory and calm whole.

The border was made about seventeen years ago, but the balance of the shapes of the plants looks easy and natural since very little pruning has been needed. In groups of shrubs which are badly planted, the plants outgrow their positions and, like the ugly sisters' feet, have to be hacked about to make them fit. They can never look quite the same again after whole sides have been chopped off to make room for a neighbour. A perfectionist might tinker with the herbaceous plants, reducing the clump of euphorbias at the front, because they do look slightly out of proportion with the rest of the group, and might possibly substitute the strong leaves of irises or hemerocallis for the agapanthus, but the bones of the border could not be bettered.

Beth Chatto's nursery is not far from this Essex garden and her influence could have had something to do with the placing of the shrubs. Mrs Chatto likes to treat flowerbeds like a flower arrangement, and to plant groups so that they make a sort of triangular shape – a shape that, in her words, 'lifts your eye upward rather than only painting a picture on the ground'. Anyone who has seen her exhibits at the Chelsea Flower Show will remember that she always builds up to a vertical plant, a sort of exclamation mark, and the principle here is the same. The plants may not be quite as subtle as Mrs Chatto's inimitable selections, but they do illustrate two more of her themes: they look good all the year round, and they are suitable for the conditions on offer which, in this case, are hot and dry.

The cypress chosen is a narrow form almost like an Italian cypress and, in winter, this evergreen and the *Viburnum × bodnantense* provide some interest. In a mild winter the cotoneasters keep their leaves on while their berries will last until the birds attack them. *Viburnum opulus*, one of Gertrude Jekyll's favourite shrubs, is good value for many months as it also follows flowers with berries.

OPPOSITE: *Shrubs in a triangular framework look effective the whole year round.*

The stephanandra's leaves colour well in autumn, so almost all the shrubs chosen provide a second helping of interest.

On a hot East Anglian day, with swallows wheeling in the summer air, there was something very settled and satisfying about this small shrubbery which is so little trouble to maintain and so lively throughout the year.

LIST OF PLANTS

  2 *Acanthus spinosus*
12 *Agapanthus campanulatus* 'Isis'
  1 *Chamaecyparis lawsoniana* 'Witzeliana'
  2 *Cistus ladanifer*
  3 *Cotoneaster × waterii*
  1 *Deutzia × elegantissima*
  7 *Euphorbia wulfenii*
  5 *Fuchsia* 'Mrs Popple'
10 *Helleborus corsicus*
  3 *Hibiscus* 'Bluebird'
  1 *Potentilla* 'Kathleen Dykes'
  1 *Rosa* 'Kathleen Harrop'
  1 *Rosa rubiginosa*
  2 *Rosa rubrifolia*
  3 *Stephanandra incisa*
  1 *Viburnum × bodnantense*
  1 *Viburnum carlcephalum*
  1 *Viburnum opulus*

Underplanting and summer bedding:
  Narcissus triandrus
  Tiarella cordifolia

LEFT: *The lime-green bottlebrush flowers of* Euphorbia wulfenii *stand out in spring.*

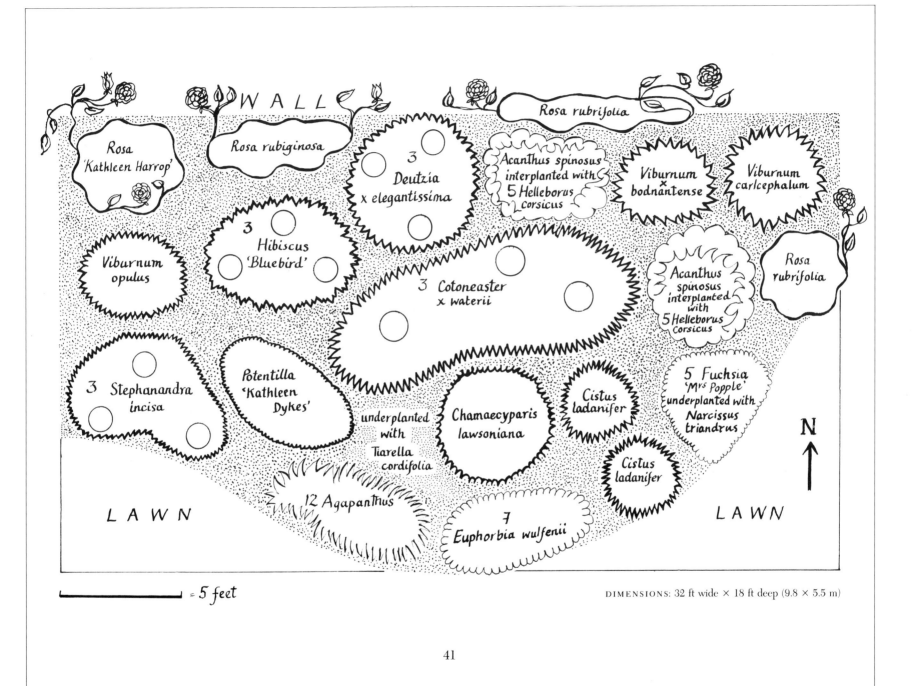

WALL

Rosa rubrifolia

Rosa 'Kathleen Harrop'

Rosa rubiginosa

3 Deutzia x elegantissima

Acanthus spinosus interplanted with 5 Helleborus corsicus

Viburnum x bodnantense

Viburnum carlcephalum

Viburnum opulus

3 Hibiscus 'Bluebird'

3 Cotoneaster x waterii

Acanthus spinosus interplanted with 5 Helleborus corsicus

Rosa rubrifolia

3 Stephanandra incisa

Potentilla 'Kathleen Dykes'

underplanted with Tiarella cordifolia

Chamaecyparis lawsoniana

Cistus ladanifer

5 Fuchsia 'Mrs Popple' underplanted with Narcissus triandrus

Cistus ladanifer

N

12 Agapanthus

7 Euphorbia wulfenii

LAWN

LAWN

= 5 feet

DIMENSIONS: 32 ft wide × 18 ft deep (9.8 × 5.5 m)

41

7

A TRADITIONAL KITCHEN GARDEN BORDER

The tradition of double flower borders dies hard. This has always been the best way to see a border, never all at a glance, but slowly as you wander between the beds, surrounded and enclosed by the sights and smells of a summer garden. Few people these days have the room or the energy for massive herbaceous borders, and the mixed border, which relies on shrubs and 'ground cover', has replaced those blazes of colour now only seen in large private or institutional gardens. The other sort of flower border which has gone out of fashion used to be seen lining the paths of kitchen gardens; backed by espaliered apples and edged with box, here grew the flowers which were picked for the house. The borders illustrated in this chapter do line the path of a modern kitchen garden where vegetables grow, and they give the effect of an old-fashioned planting which is now rarely seen. Set in a walled enclosure, the beds extend as far again as the length of border shown in the

photograph, beyond an archway of trained pear trees which marks the crossing of two paths at the centre of the garden.

The owner did not choose the conventional box edging for the beds on the grounds that it was too expensive, that the clipping would have been too much work and that it would harbour snails. This decision has not been regretted. However, the espaliered apples which would have backed the border in an older garden were also eliminated and this has proved a mistake. Very loose plantings of soft flowers like poppies, cornflowers, peonies and daisies need firm outlines to contain them if they are not to look a mess. A gravel path and a series of six iron arches along the sixty-foot length of the garden have not been able to formalize the design sufficiently and the owner now plans to remedy this, perhaps with a three-tiered fence of thornless blackberries rather than the traditional fruit trees. To add more structure to the flimsy planting of

flowers, artichokes and the odd clump of rhubarb have been included, as well as a few tall, old-fashioned Bourbon roses. It is a planting which owes something to Beatrix Potter and a lot to Monet. Flowers are crammed into every available space throughout the year, resulting in the sort of gardening which is probably more work than most people would enjoy.

Early in the year masses of tulips in rainbow colours and a few hyacinths appear above the emerging leaves of the perennials, at the same time as the pears are in blossom. The bulbs are planted deep and left in the ground all year; as the soil is fairly light, this seems to suit them, but on heavier soils, crown imperials might be better value for early colour and height in the beds. Every year patches of wallflowers,

OPPOSITE: *Columbines, daisies, sweet williams and peonies may not be the most rarefied sort of flowers but they create a traditional effect in a kitchen garden.*

Brompton stocks and sweet williams are fitted into any gaps. Cornflowers and Shirley poppies are sown in September of the previous year and clumps of these are placed wherever there is room. Annuals are selected because this sort of garden changes from year to year and although the peonies, roses and delphiniums are more or less permanent fixtures, along with the odd shrub like southernwood or the winter flowering daphne, the character of the border is flowery and transient, which can only be achieved by a liberal use of annuals and biennials.

Around the middle of July the cranesbills, delphiniums, violas and daisies are cut back and given plenty of water and liquid feed to encourage them to flower again. The annuals and biennials, such as the cornflowers and sweet williams, are pulled out and replaced with varieties for later on in the year like cosmos or love-in-a-mist, and also with perennials like dahlia 'Bishop of Llandaff' and Michaelmas daisies, which are kept in a reserve plot. All these need watering copiously if they are to survive being transplanted in the heat of the summer, but a week to ten days usually sees them safely established.

It is not worth attempting to grow this continual display of flowers without a back-up plot where plants can be grown and kept in reserve to fill the gaps when others stop flowering. The border is at its best until the end

OPPOSITE: *Shirley poppies grow into bigger plants from a September sowing. The old white 'Mrs Sinkins' pink is hard to beat, even though it dies disgracefully.*

Early in the year tulips appear through the leaves of peonies.

of June; the roses then act as a distraction while the flowering patches have their annual change-over, when the border can look a little thin, but by the end of July it has recovered again and emerges in stronger colours, with pink and purple Michaelmas daisies and red dahlias carrying on until the autumn frosts.

It is not an easy border to manage for if flowers are to be kept going they must be regularly deadheaded and such intensive cultivation needs plenty of feeding and watering to keep it in peak condition. Added to this, many of the plants need careful staking and some, like the artichokes, will need dividing annually and spraying if they are not to fall foul of the blackfly. Although this appears to be an artless confusion of flowers it needs very careful and skilled control if it is not to appear messy or skimpy. For all these reasons this kind of planting is quite rare in gardens nowadays, which makes it all the more attractive when it succeeds.

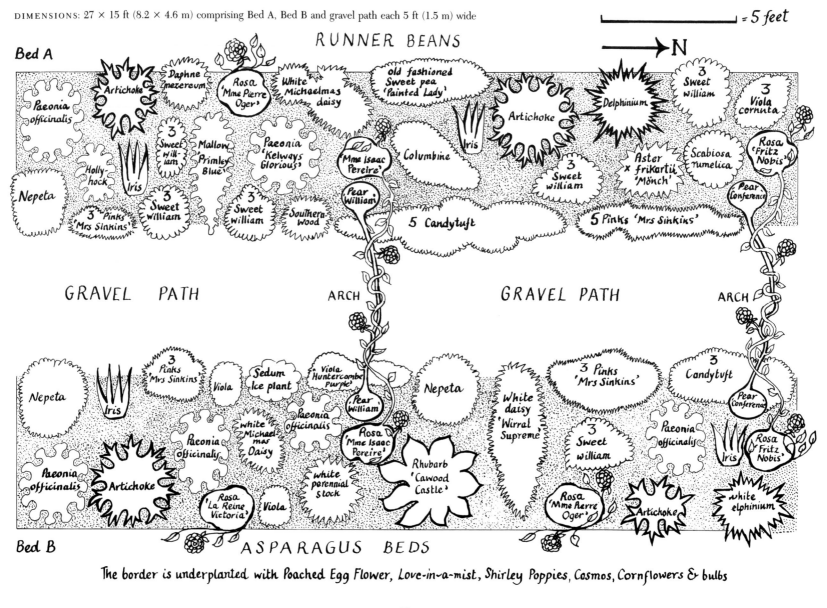

DIMENSIONS: 27 × 15 ft (8.2 × 4.6 m) comprising Bed A, Bed B and gravel path each 5 ft (1.5 m) wide

= 5 feet

N

RUNNER BEANS

Bed A

Paeonia officinalis

Artichoke

Daphne mezereum

Rosa 'Mme Pierre Oger'

White Michaelmas daisy

old fashioned Sweet pea 'Painted Lady'

Artichoke

Delphinium

3 Sweet william

3 Viola cornuta

Hollyhock

3 Sweet william

Iris

Mallow 'Primley Blue'

Paeonia Kelways Glorious'

Mme Isaac Pereire'

Columbine

Iris

3 Sweet william

Aster × frikartii 'Mönch'

Scabiosa rumelica

Rosa 'Fritz Nobis'

Nepeta

3 Pinks 'Mrs Sinkins'

3 Sweet william

3 Sweet william

Southernwood

Pear William

5 Candytuft

5 Pinks 'Mrs Sinkins'

Pear Conference

GRAVEL PATH

ARCH

GRAVEL PATH

ARCH

Nepeta

Iris

3 Pinks 'Mrs Sinkins'

Viola

Sedum Ice plant

Viola Huntercombe Purple

Nepeta

White daisy 'Wirral Supreme'

3 Pinks 'Mrs Sinkins'

3 Candytuft

white Michaelmas Daisy

Paeonia officinalis

Pear William

3 Sweet william

Paeonia officinalis

Pear Conference

Paeonia officinalis

Paeonia officinalis

Rosa 'Mme Isaac Pereire'

Iris

Rosa 'Fritz Nobis'

Paeonia officinalis

Artichoke

white perennial stock

Rhubarb 'Cawood Castle'

Rosa 'Mme Pierre Oger'

Artichoke

white elphinium

Rosa 'La Reine Victoria'

Viola

Bed B

ASPARAGUS BEDS

The border is underplanted with Poached Egg Flower, Love-in-a-mist, Shirley Poppies, Cosmos, Cornflowers & bulbs

46

LIST OF PLANTS

BED A

1 *Althaea rosea* (hollyhock, single)
7 Aquilegia in variety (columbine)
1 *Artemisia arbrotanum* (southernwood)
2 Artichoke 'Gros Vert de Laon'
1 *Aster divaricatus* (white Michaelmas daisy)
1 *Aster × frikartii* 'Mönch' (blue Michaelmas daisy)
1 *Daphne mezereum*
1 *Delphinium* Belladonna Hybrid
8 *Dianthus* 'Mrs Sinkins' (pinks)
5 *Iberis sempervirens* (candytuft)
6 *Iris* 'Jane Phillips'
1 *Lathyrus odoratus* 'Painted Lady' (old fashioned sweet pea)
1 *Malva* 'Primley Blue' (mallow)
1 *Nepeta* 'Souvenir d'André Chaudron' (catmint)
1 *Paeonia* 'Kelways Glorious'
1 *Paeonia officinalis*
1 Pear 'Conference'

1 Pear 'William's Bon Chrétien'
1 *Rosa* 'Fritz Nobis'
1 *Rosa* 'Mme Isaac Pereire'
1 *Rosa* 'Mme Pierre Oger'
1 *Scabiosa rumelica*
15 Sweet william
3 *Viola cornuta*

BED B

2 Artichoke 'Gros Vert de Laon'
1 *Aster divaricatus* (white Michaelmas daisy)
2 *Chrysanthemum* 'Wirral Supreme' (white daisy)
1 Delphinium (white)
6 *Dianthus* 'Mrs Sinkins' (pinks)
3 *Iberis sempervirens* (candytuft)
6 *Iris* 'Jane Phillips'
1 *Matthiola* 'White Perennial Stock'
2 *Nepeta* 'Souvenir d'André Chaudron' (catmint)
4 *Paeonia officinalis* (underplanted with *Geranium* 'Buxton's Blue')
1 Pear 'Conference'
1 Pear 'William's Bon Chrétien'

1 Rhubarb 'Cawood Castle'
1 *Rosa* 'Fritz Nobis'
1 *Rosa* 'La Reine Victoria'
1 *Rosa* 'Mme Isaac Pereire'
1 *Rosa* 'Mme Pierre Oger'
1 *Sedum* 'Autumn Joy' (ice plant)
3 Sweet william
2 *Viola cornuta*
3 *Viola* 'Huntercombe Purple'

Both beds underplanted with:
    Cosmos; Love-in-a-mist; Shirley poppies;
    Cornflowers; Poached egg flower; Tulip
    'General de Wet'; Tulip 'Peach Blossom';
    Tulip 'Clara Butt'; *Fritillaria imperialis* (crown imperials).

In reserve:
    Chrysanthemum rubellum 'Clara Curtis';
    Michaelmas daisies; *Aster lateriflorus*; *Dahlia* 'Bishop of Llandaff'.

8

ALL YEAR INTEREST FOR A GRAVEL FORECOURT

The drives and entrances to houses are places where people do not linger. Where the cars are parked is not a place for contemplation, so the best sort of planting for such areas is one which makes a bold impression all through the year. For sheltered areas in a warm southern garden this collection of plants looks sunny and welcoming even in the winter. The southerly aspect and free-draining gravel soil suit shrubs that might not be hardy in less favoured positions, but the principles of planting could be the same further north if substitutes were made.

The bed is backed by an arc of large shrubs which are all (apart from the lilac) at their best in winter. The garrya and the pittosporums would not succeed in colder gardens. Garrya looks particularly unprepossessing after a hard winter has made its evergreen leaves and long-tailed catkins turn brown, which then remain brown all summer. Removing these is a major task, so it is not a shrub to grow in an important place if the climate is hard. A good holly – 'J. C. van Tol' perhaps, or the one with yellow berries called 'Amber' – would provide an evergreen background and could grow as a bush rather than a tree. In place of the pittosporum, *Euonymus* 'Macrophyllus Albus' might do. It would not look quite as refined as the designer's choice does in this garden, but would make the same sort of show at a distance. It would be important, in a similar planting, to dedicate at least half of the bed to winter effect, bearing in mind that some of the evergreens and subshrubs chosen would not be suitable for colder gardens. Impressus is one of the hardiest of the ceanothuses but in the north an osmanthus might be better. *Escallonia* 'Iveyi' is a lovely shrub with high-gloss leaves and hawthorn-like flowers, but it is not reliable and one of the ordinary forms of escallonia with smaller leaves might have to be substituted in a colder garden. The salvias and grey foliage plants at the front of the border might also cause problems, but there are plenty of alternatives. More clumps of hellebores or hart's-tongue ferns, or groups of box could all make low patches of green for long periods in the year. Splashes of purple could be provided by the dwarf *Berberis thunbergii* 'Atropurpurea Nana', or by heather for those who like it and who garden on acid soil.

The important thing about a planting like this is to concentrate on making the leaves, rather than the flowers, produce the effect which provides bold sweeps of colour and not too much change throughout the year. The leaves and shapes of shrubs create a solid, settled pattern and the few flowers which do appear are a bonus, but are never vital to the

OPPOSITE: *Foxgloves and yellow flowers against the grey santolina provide colour in a border which is designed for all-year interest.*

LEFT: *The woolly grey mullein from Greece has sulphur-yellow flowers and looks like a dignified exclamation mark.*

LIST OF PLANTS

7 *Agapanthus* 'Headbourne Hybrids'
5 *Ajuga reptans* 'Burgundy Glow' (purple bugle)
8 *Alchemilla mollis*
2 *Artemisia* 'Powis Castle'
1 *Ceanothus impressus*
3 *Cheiranthus* 'Bowles Mauve' (wallflower)
4 *Cheiranthus* 'Harpur Crewe'
1 *Cornus alba* 'Elegantissima'
1 *Cornus mas* (cornelian cherry)
1 *Cotoneaster horizontalis* 'Variegatus'
1 *Cotoneaster* × *wateri*
3 *Dahlia* 'Fascination'
2 *Escallonia* 'Iveyi'
1 *Garrya elliptica*
3 *Helleborus corsicus* (hellebores)
1 *Hypericum* × *moseranum* 'Tricolor'
7 *Mentha* × *rotundifolia* 'Variegata' (variegated
    apple mint)
3 *Pittosporum* 'Garnettii'
1 *Robinia pseudoacacia* 'Frisia' (golden acacia)
3 *Salvia officinalis* 'Icterina' (golden sage)
4 *Salvia officinalis* 'Purpurascens' (purple sage)
1 *Sambucus nigra* 'Aurea' (golden elder)
3 *Santolina virens*
1 *Syringa vulgaris* 'Firmament' (lilac)
5 *Verbascum* 'Broussa' (mullein)

Underplanting and summer bedding:
    Digitalis × *mertonensis*
    Digitalis purpurea (foxgloves)
    Hedera helix (common ivy)

structure. Flowers among shrubs need to be of a good size and an easy temperament. Foxgloves are always acceptable and so is brunnera, which has flowers like forget-me-nots and giant leaves that last all summer. The little known six-foot tobacco plant, *Nicotiana sylvestris*, as well as honesty in both its ordinary and its variegated forms, will not look out of place, nor will the many lilies which are tall enough to stand with shrubs. The flowers to choose are the ones which can be seen from afar or in a hurry. Like the rest of the bed, they should not depend on close inspection to be appreciated.

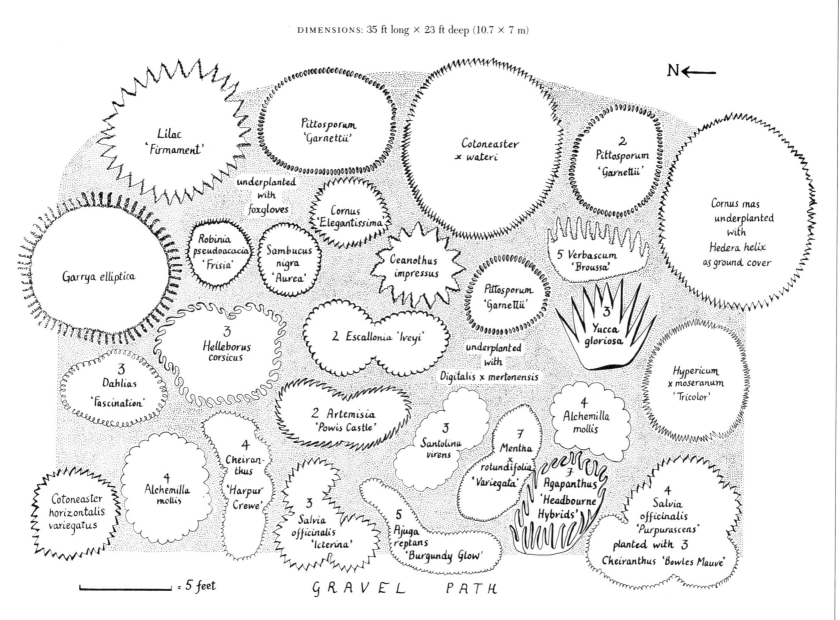

N ←

Lilac 'Firmament'

Pittosporum 'Garnettii'

Cotoneaster × wateri

2 Pittosporum 'Garnettii'

Cornus mas underplanted with Hedera helix as ground cover

underplanted with foxgloves

Cornus 'Elegantissima'

Robinia pseudoacacia 'Frisia'

Sambucus nigra 'Aurea'

Ceanothus impressus

Pittosporum 'Garnettii'

5 Verbascum 'Broussa'

Garrya elliptica

3 Helleborus corsicus

2 Escallonia 'Iveyi'

underplanted with Digitalis × mertonensis

3 Yucca gloriosa

Hypericum × moseranum 'Tricolor'

3 Dahlias 'Fascination'

2 Artemisia 'Powis Castle'

3 Santolina virens

7 Mentha × rotundifolia 'Variegata'

4 Alchemilla mollis

4 Cheiranthus 'Harpur Crewe'

7 Agapanthus 'Headbourne Hybrids'

Cotoneaster horizontalis variegatus

4 Alchemilla mollis

3 Salvia officinalis 'Icterina'

5 Ajuga reptans 'Burgundy Glow'

4 Salvia officinalis 'Purpurascens' planted with 3 Cheiranthus 'Bowles Mauve'

⊢——⊣ = 5 feet

GRAVEL PATH

51

9

Unusual Plants for a Shaded Wall Border

This shady border crowded with rare plants does not look dull for a single day of the year. The greenery partly obscures the windows, which might not be so desirable if the rooms behind were living rooms, but this is the back door to a house with an open and formal façade and the only outlook the plants mask is from the cloakroom or the hall. Such lushness surrounds a house with mystery, and even in winter there is always something to look at as people arrive and depart. Leaf shapes are strong, without suggesting the heavy hand of the landscaper, and colour is subdued. The secondary entrance to a house is a good place for a collection of plants, ones that can bear close examination and which change with the seasons. It's a place to put favourite plants where they can be supervised and admired several times a day. This border is the antithesis of the strong impact created by John Brookes's forecourt planting (see Chapter 8) and is a place to linger even on the coldest day.

The neutral soil is not particularly good but it has been improved by plenty of compost. The sun never reaches the flowerbed at all but, with so much shelter, the climate is not a trial and everything in the border thrives in shade. The most surprising plant to find in such a dark place is *Bupleurum fruticosum*, the evergreen which grows on dry sunny hills in the Mediterranean. Its sea-green leaves and yellowish flowers look sombre and discreet in the corner angle of the house. It does not seem to mind the lack of sun, which only goes to show that it is worth trying anything anywhere if you have plants to spare and the time to experiment. Hydrangeas are a feature of this border and they look magnificent at the end of summer. A garden with acid soil would bring out the blue of *Hydrangea* 'Mariesii'. *Hydrangea* 'Quadricolor' is a variety of this plant rarely offered for sale, but the form 'Tricolor' which has a three-tone variation in its leaf colour, rather than the four shades

found in 'Quadricolor', is widely available. Ferns are also important here. The male fern *Dryopteris filix-mas* is normally seen in wild gardens, but it is quite distinguished enough to include in a flowerbed. Across the path from it grows the lady fern (*Athyrium filix-femina*) and the painted fern from Japan, which likes a sheltered position. It is one of the most intriguing plants of all but is not very easy to find. Another plant which is difficult to come by is the hellebore 'Nigristern', a marvellous cross between two types of hellebore, producing enormous glossy leaves and coffee-saucer-sized flowers. The *Helleborus orientalis* is a good yellow seedling found in the garden. In a place like this where it is possible to keep a close watch on rare plants, it is worth hunting down

OPPOSITE: *Good forms of foliage plants jostle for supremacy in this shaded house-wall border.* Acanthus perlingii *has the same statuesque flower as the commoner sort, but has broader and better leaves.*

the best forms. But among the uncommon plants are a few familiars. White campanulas, as well as a white variegated honesty, seed themselves about the bed and are only removed if they interfere with something else. The white phlox is the old, unimproved form which smells better than modern sorts, and the Solomon's seal is the giant form.

BELOW: *Hydrangea 'Quadricolor' has four shades of colour in its leaves and is a variety of* Hydrangea *'Mariesii'.*

Everything is of the best and when I suggested to the owner that substitutes might have to be found for some of the uncommon plants, it was obvious that alternatives would not be acceptable. Things like *Begonia sutherlandii*, the only begonia which is hardy in England, may not be in everyone's garden centre, but the reason this bed is interesting for so many months of the year is because infinite care and trouble has been taken to find the best forms of all the plants grown.

LIST OF PLANTS

BED A
1 *Astrantia major* 'Shaggy'
1 *Athyrium filix-femina* 'Percristatum' (fern)
1 *Begonia sutherlandii*
1 *Epimedium × versicolor* 'Alba'
1 *Hydrangea macrophylla* 'Beauté Vendômoise'
5 *Lamium maculatum* 'Nancy's White' (white dead nettle)
1 *Osmanthus delavayi*
1 *Phygelius aequalis* 'Yellow Trumpet' (figwort)
3 *Polygonatum canaliculatum* (Solomon's seal)
2 *Tiarella cordifolia*
1 *Viola septentrionalis*

BED B
1 *Acanthus perlingii*
5 *Anemone rivularis*
2 *Astrantia major* 'Shaggy'
1 *Athyrium nipponicum* 'Pictum' (painted fern)
1 *Athyrium vidalii* (fern)
1 *Bupleurum fruticosum*
1 *Campanula persicifolia* 'Alba'
2 *Chrysanthemum parthenium* 'Rowallane'
1 *Clematis viticella*
1 *Cyrtomium falcatum* (fern)
1 *Dryopteris filix-mas* (fern)
1 *Helleborus* 'Nigristern'
1 *Helleborus orientalis*
1 *Hemerocallis* 'Whichford' (day lily)
1 *Hosta fortunei* 'Albopicta'
1 *Hosta sieboldiana*
1 *Hydrangea arborescens* 'Grandiflora'
1 *Hydrangea* 'Mariesii'
1 *Hydrangea* 'Quadricolor'
1 *Lonicera japonica* 'Aureoreticulata'
1 *Lysimachia clethroides* (loosestrife)
3 *Phlox maculata* 'Old Rectory White'
1 *Rosa alba regalis* 'Great Maiden's Blush'
1 *Rosa* 'May Queen'
1 *Sanguinaria canadensis* 'Flore Pleno' (double bloodroot)

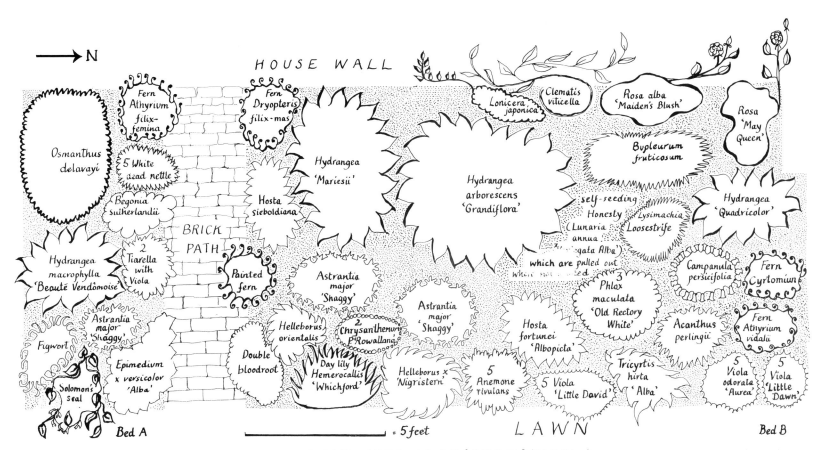

→ N

HOUSE WALL

Osmanthus delavayi

Fern Athyrium filix-femina

5 White dead nettle

Begonia sutherlandii

Fern Dryopteris filix-mas

Hosta sieboldiana

Hydrangea 'Mariesii'

Lonicera japonica

Clematis viticella

Rosa alba 'Maiden's Blush'

Rosa 'May Queen'

Bupleurum fruticosum

Hydrangea arborescens 'Grandiflora'

self-seeding Honesty (Lunaria annua Variegata Alba') which are pulled out when not wanted

Lysimachia Loosestrife

Hydrangea 'Quadricolor'

BRICK PATH

Hydrangea macrophylla 'Beauté Vendômoise'

2 Tiarella with Viola

Painted fern

Astrantia major 'Shaggy'

Astrantia major 'Shaggy'

3 Phlox maculata 'Old Rectory White'

Campanula persicifolia

Fern Cyrtomium

Astrantia major 'Shaggy'

Epimedium × versicolor 'Alba'

Helleborus orientalis

2 Chrysanthemum 'Rowallane'

Hosta fortunei 'Albopicta'

Acanthus perlingii

Fern Athyrium vidalii

Figwort

Double bloodroot

Day lily Hemerocallis 'Whichford'

Helleborus × 'Nigristern'

5 Anemone rivulans

5 Viola 'Little David'

Tricyrtis hirta 'Alba'

5 Viola odorata 'Aurea'

5 Viola 'Little Dawn'

Solomon's seal

Bed A

═ 5 feet

LAWN

Bed B

DIMENSIONS: Bed A 11 × 5 ft (3.4 × 1.5 m) Bed B 11 × 20 ft (3.4 × 6.1 m)

1 *Tricyrtis hirta* 'Alba'
5 *Viola* 'Little David'
5 *Viola* 'Little Dawn'
5 *Viola odorata* 'Aurea'

Underplanting and summer bedding:
   Arisaema japonicum
   Fritillaria meleagris 'Alba'

Fritillaria pontica
Galanthus plicatus 'Warham' (snowdrop)
Leucojum vernum 'Warham' (snowflake)
Lunaria annua 'Variegata Alba' (self-seeding
   honesty)
Narcissus 'Dove Wings'
Narcissus × *accidentalis*
Trillium grandiflorum

55

10

EASY ALPINES FOR A CIRCULAR BED

Gardens that are filled with plants and flowers bought on impulse, which have been chosen for their instant and often bright colour and brought home in full flower, tend not to be as effective as those which have been more carefully planned. This bed owes its success not to its owner's failure to resist temptation, but to the formal framework which surrounds the impulse-buys. Even the most disparate collection can be dignified by such a distinguished setting and anyone who likes the idea of picking up a plant at the Chelsea Flower Show and another in the market and another from a friend in order to create a low patchwork of pretty and easy flowers, could not find a better way of displaying them than this.

In this arrangement the urn is important but too expensive to copy. There are tolerable reproductions now on the market, but a corkscrew of topiary box, or even of quickthorn or lonicera, would make an effective substitute for the stonework. A more conventional plant-ing for this round bed in full sun might have been lavender or a formal bedding scheme, but I doubt it would look so unusual or so pretty. The bed is at its best in spring when pools of colour surround the eighteenth-century urn. Even earlier than the trailing rock plants, which are out at the end of spring and in early summer, the little sun-loving bulbs appear, such as *Crocus sieberi* and *Iris reticulata* or *I. histrioides*. These flower in February and March and could be followed by species tulips: either the lady tulip, *Tulipa clusiana*, with its cherry-red and white petals, or *T. praestans*, the scarlet tulip with several flowers to a stem. St Brigid anemones would be suitable, too, and any of these bulbs would extend the flowering season.

All the plants chosen have to like sharp drainage and full sun. The heat reflected off the bricks in a good summer is strong and suits plants which come from the Alps, where the summers are hot and the winds are dry.

Alpines loathe damp for, at home, they are used to winters under a blanket of snow which keeps them dry and dark. Good drainage will remind them of their native land. The violas included here will probably not be happy throughout the summer unless they are given some water because, although they can stand sun, they prefer moist, humus-rich soil if they are to flower well. Violas can literally flower themselves to death so need to be cut back, fed and watered when they show signs of exhaustion, which is usually about the middle of July in the south of England. This enforced rest, together with plenty of water and nourishment, soon gets them going again and they will then flower until the end of the summer. The helianthemums also need to be cut back after flowering to prevent them from growing too untidy.

OPPOSITE: *Small rock plants are irresistible in spring. Pink aubrietas and white candytuft are kept in check by a formal layout.*

A pastiche knot garden without the fuss of small beds gives a focal point to the lawn of an old house.

The concentration on spring effect means that, apart from the violas and helianthemums and the occasional thyme, there is not much to look at after the early display is over. Some plants which might be included for later in the year are the small, pale version of St John's wort, or hypericum, which is rarely seen, but ought to be better known. *Hypericum olympicum* 'Citrinum' is a miniature shrub with sulphur yellow flowers for three months on end. *Silene schafta* 'Abbotswood' is another perennial which lasts almost as long and has pink flowers on floppy stems. Some of the dianthus chosen here might resent dust-dry conditions, but the smaller, pink *Dianthus deltoides*, which is also in bloom for several weeks, does not seem to mind a hot place and this too would be a useful plant to grow in similar conditions. The bed could be given an extra fillip by sowing an annual as ordinary as nasturtium among the more permanent rock plants. 'Empress of India' is the neatest form with bluish leaves and lacquer-red flowers, but those who find red too bright could opt for a pale yellow trailing form. All nasturtiums like hot, dry, poor soil and this is the sort of place where they would thrive. All the planting suggestions for this circular bed could be adopted for any rockery or bed of alpines.

LIST OF PLANTS

1 *Anthemis cupaniana*
1 *Armeria maritima* (thrift)
2 *Aubrieta* 'Bressingham Pink'
2 *Aubrieta* 'Dr Mules'
2 *Dianthus* 'Doris' (pinks)
1 *Dianthus* 'Prudence' (pinks)
1 *Dianthus* 'White Ladies' (pinks)
2 *Helianthemum* 'Ben Hope'
1 *Helianthemum* 'The Bride'
2 *Iberis sempervirens* (candytuft)
1 *Lithospermum* 'Grace Ward'
2 *Phlox subulata* 'G. F. Wilson'

1 *Potentilla alba*
1 *Potentilla* 'Longacre'
1 *Potentilla nitida* 'Rubra'
4 *Saponaria officinalis*
1 *Thymus* × *citriodorus* 'Silver Queen'
1 *Thymus vulgaris* (common thyme)
1 *Viola cornuta* 'Belmont Blue'
1 *Viola* 'Jackanapes'
2 *Viola labradorica*
2 *Viola tricolor* (heartsease)

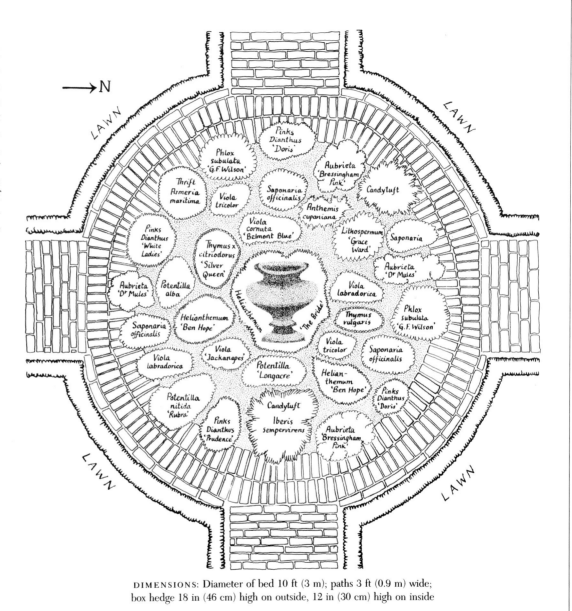

DIMENSIONS: Diameter of bed 10 ft (3 m); paths 3 ft (0.9 m) wide; box hedge 18 in (46 cm) high on outside, 12 in (30 cm) high on inside

59

11

SILVER SHRUBS AGAINST A BRICK FAÇADE

Architectural purists disapprove of planting directly against period houses; gardeners find it irresistible especially if, as in this garden, the façade provides a south-facing wall to shelter tender things. Eight hundred feet up on the Berkshire Downs, high winds and late springs can make gardening difficult, but even in places which suffer the worst climates, there are generally one or two sheltered pockets in the angles of buildings or against good walls, so it would be a shame not to take advantage of the microclimate which they offer. The border here is very narrow and the general impression is of neat domes and pools of silvery plants pinning the house to the gravel, while on its walls creepers are allowed to grow in sweet disorder. Against brick the choice of colour can be more limiting than against stone: yellow can clash and so can pinks with strong magenta tones. However, the pale colours chosen here are a clever foil for the house and there is plenty of evergreen for winter.

It is reassuring to see that even in gardens full of rare plants, there are certain old favourites which can compete with the latest in horticultural crazes. The classic plants here are *Rosa* 'New Dawn', *Clematis montana* and the winter-flowering jasmine, all of which ought to be familiar to many people and are sometimes scorned for that reason. There is little to be said for choosing difficult, rare plants in preference to easy ones, unless you happen to like them better. *Jasminum nudiflorum* will grow on north walls in the poorest soils which means it is often denied a better position; it deserves an important place in any garden because there is nothing prettier than those showers of golden stars throughout five long months of winter.

In this planting, with a good spread of interest for all seasons of the year, there are other winter flowers beside the jasmine. *Iris* 'Mary Barnard' is late to flower, but is a good, dark form of the winter-flowering iris, and the white *Daphne mezereum* is out by the end of February. In all but the worst winters there are some clumps of silver to admire and the leaves of the cyclamen are always decorative. In warm spells the gay perennial wallflower *Cheiranthus* 'Bowles Mauve' can be relied on to put out a few purple sprays, so the border never looks completely bare of flowers. In late spring and summer there is a feeling of abundance from traditional plants like roses, honeysuckle and clematis as well as from the unusual actinidia which looks like a large vine. Actinidia produces the New Zealand kiwi fruit but will only do so in very hot summers.

Some of the plants might be difficult to find. *Cirsium rivulare* is an attractive thistle, but it could be replaced by *Morina longifolia* which is increasingly available and has the advantage of being evergreen. Accept no substitute for

OPPOSITE: *Pools of grey foliage lie at the feet of a classical house anchoring it to the ground without interfering with the architecture.*

Crepis incana, which is a lovely long-flowering perennial that ought to be better known. It has pink dandelion flowers for weeks on end and makes a pretty edge to any border. *Salvia argentea* has great silver-felted leaves which like bone-dry conditions and it would not be happy anywhere except in a hot, well-drained site. Marrubium, which looks like the better known ballota, is well worth finding and the annual omphalodes ought to seed itself once it has been introduced to a garden, so it is odd that it is not more often seen.

This is the sort of border where, because of the risks attached to growing semi-hardy things in an unkind climate, there is quite a turnover of plants and, for this reason, it would not be a planting to imitate if you dislike change. Exciting gardens are not static and the best gardeners take chances all the time. They take precautions, too, and keep a stock of spare plants in a frame or greenhouse to fill the gaps after a bad winter. Nevertheless, gardeners who specialize in unusual plants will always welcome the chance to grow something different when other things have failed. In this garden there is a permanent backdrop of more reliable plants to cover up for the experiments which turn out to be disasters, which is a sensible plan for anyone who likes the idea of trying new things but who also enjoys a conventionally pretty garden.

LEFT: *Climbers are allowed to run riot against the façade of this restrained house giving it a romantic and secretive air.*
RIGHT: *'Bowles Mauve', the perennial wallflower, is in bloom for about three months but is at its best in spring.*

63

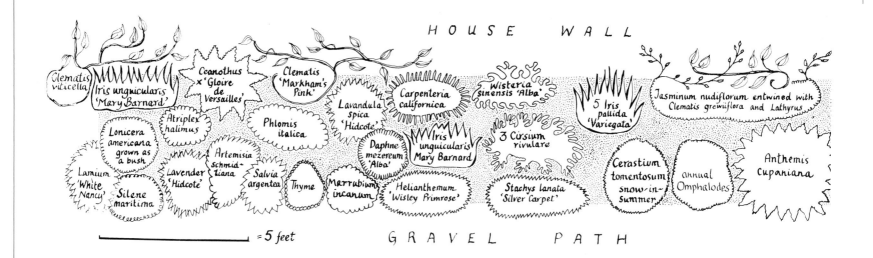

H O U S E   W A L L

= 5 feet

G R A V E L   P A T H

LIST OF PLANTS

1 *Actinidia chinensis* (kiwi fruit)
2 *Anthemis cupaniana*
1 *Artemisia schmidtiana*
1 *Asplenium scolopendrium* (hart's-tongue fern)
1 *Atriplex halimus*
1 *Carpenteria californica*
1 *Ceanothus* × 'Autumnal Blue'
1 *Ceanothus* × 'Gloire de Versailles'

1 *Cerastium tomentosum* (snow-in-summer)
2 *Cheiranthus* 'Bowles Mauve' (perennial
    wallflower)
3 *Cirsium rivulare*
1 *Clematis alpina* 'Columbine'
1 *Clematis alpina* 'Ruby'
1 *Clematis* 'Etoile Rose'
1 *Clematis grewiiflora* (possible substitute
    Clematis rehderana)
1 *Clematis* 'Markham's Pink'

1 *Clematis montana*
1 *Clematis viticella* 'Alba Luxurians'
5 *Colchicum* 'Princess Astrid'
5 *Colchicum speciosum* 'Album'
3 *Crepis incana* (pink dandelion)
7 *Cyclamen hederifolium*
1 *Daphne mezereum* 'Alba'
1 *Daphne* 'Somerset'
1 *Hebe* 'Cranleigh Gem'
1 *Hebe pinguifolia* 'Pagei'

Bed B 12 × 4 ft (3.7 × 1.2 m)   Path 4 ft (1.2 m) wide

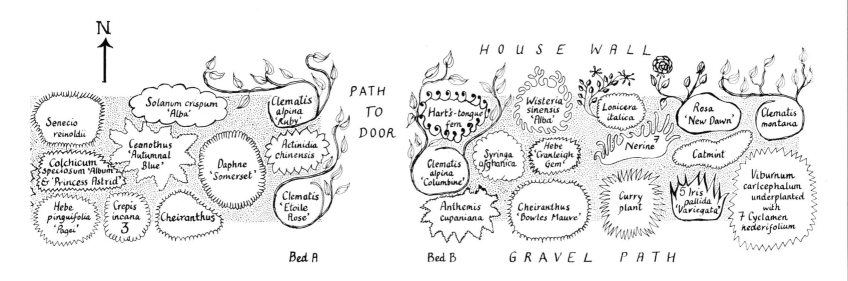

1 *Helianthemum* 'Wisley Primrose' (rockrose)
1 *Helichrysum serotinum* (curry plant)
10 *Iris pallida* 'Variegata'
7 *Iris unguicularis* 'Mary Barnard'
1 *Jasminum nudiflorum*
1 *Lamium* 'White Nancy'
1 *Lathyrus* 'Rose Queen'
2 *Lavandula spica* 'Hidcote' (lavender)
1 *Lonicera × americana* (grown as bush)
1 *Lonicera etrusca* (honeysuckle)

1 *Marrubium incanum*
1 *Nepeta* 'Six Hills Giant' (catmint)
7 *Nerine bowdenii*
1 *Omphalodes linifolia*
1 *Phlomis italica* (pink sage)
1 *Rosa* 'New Dawn'
1 *Salvia argentea*
1 *Senecio reinoldii* (possible substitute *Senecio monroi*)
1 *Silene maritima*

1 *Solanum crispum* 'Alba' (Chilean potato tree)
1 *Stachys lanata* 'Silver Carpet' (large form)
1 *Syringa afghanica* (lilac)
1 *Thymus × citriodoros* 'Silver Queen'
1 *Viburnum carlcephalum*
2 *Wisteria sinensis* 'Alba'

65

12

A WEEKEND GARDENER'S BORDER

Weekend gardeners have little time for the attentions which more regular cultivators can practise so, when they are not full of weeds, weekenders' flowerbeds tend to be full of shrubs and easy ground cover, leaving a general impression that is either dull or unkempt. Finding a patch of flowery colour in a part-time garden which is neither of these things is rare. The planting shown here in a cold cottage garden on clay was based on a red and pink colour scheme that was devised to go with a *Rosa rubrifolia* and a pink spiraea which a previous owner had left behind. It is often worth retaining one or two mature plants to give a new planting some height and character, and it can make designing a border easier if there are some restrictions on colour, so picking out a couple of basic plants and building round them, as this owner has done, is a sensible plan. Often the key plants change as the planting matures and here the original pair has ceased to be important. Instead, the

bed is dominated in June by clouds of white flowers from the crambe and a mass of wild marguerites which help to keep the weeds down, as well as plenty of pink from roses and cranesbills to set the cottage garden mood. Over the years plants have been what their owner describes as 'pushed around', but the colour scheme has not altered. One year a scarlet rose 'Fountains' was tried next to the magenta 'Roseraie de l'Hay' which was instantly recognized as a ghastly mistake. Winter brainwaves found in the catalogues at a time when colour is scarce can often turn out to be disasters when the order arrives and all gardeners make slips like this. The important thing is to be able to recognize the failures and to remove them if they interfere with the masterplan. There are places where a clash of scarlet and pink might work, but this was not one of them.

Although the border is at its best in June, when it looks like a flimsy riot of colour, there

is a strong winter skeleton to stand through the months when the flowers are gone. Two skyrocket junipers and a winter flowering cherry make a triangle of interest to view from the house and in most years there should be some colour until late in the year from the red in the stems of the *rubrifolia* rose as well as from the berberis and the purple sages, with perhaps some hips from the *rugosa* rose. This winter effect could be stepped up a little by planting *Cyclamen coum* and *Cyclamen hederifolium* under the kolkwitzia, the cotinus and the weigela which would give them the shade which they like. Cyclamen and aconites are always a possible underplanting for summer shrubs which are bare in winter, but which become dense enough to cover the bulbs when

OPPOSITE: *A jumble of flowers in simple shapes provides a cottage-garden mood for the city-dwelling weekend gardener and is not too much trouble to look after.*

the sun shines. It is, however, better to keep them with plants that need no manure, rather than under things like roses which prefer a rich diet. There ought also to be room in a bed like this for plenty of spring bulbs.

'Rembrandt' tulips and familiar varieties like the pink 'Clara Butt', as well as pale narcissi (not too much yellow), would be in keeping with the colour scheme. The peony

Aquilegias come in all shades and give a light and flowery look early in the year.

leaves, which emerge at the same time as the early tulips, provide more red as they open and they can look good with the bricky red of crown imperials, which always do well on heavy soil and give some height to the bed early in the season. At the moment, in late spring, the border is full of columbines in pale yellow, cream, white and apricot. With such pale colours and those of the self-sown violas and flowering wild strawberries, it might be better to delay the strong colours until the summer. In autumn there is also some interest, which has been concentrated on the end of the bed nearest the house. Clumps of pink Korean chrysanthemums appear at the same time as the second flowering of the roses 'Altissimo' and 'Mme Isaac Pereire', against a background of crimson-leaved berberis and purple-leaved sage and in front of the original *rubrifolia* rose. When I see a bed like this I always think it would be fun to devote one part to each of the seasons, having an autumn corner as the owner has done here, but building up spring, summer and winter effects in the other quarters.

LIST OF PLANTS

 1 *Althaea rosea* (hollyhock)
11 *Anaphalis triplinervis*
 2 *Artemisia* 'Powis Castle'
 1 *Artemisia* 'Silver Queen'
 1 *Berberis thunbergii* 'Rose Glow'
 1 *Ceanothus* 'Repens'
15 *Chrysanthemum rubellum* 'Clara Curtis'
 1 *Cotinus coggyria* 'Foliis Purpureis'
 1 *Crambe cordifolia*

 7 *Dianthus* 'Mrs Sinkins' (pink)
 1 *Dorycnium suffruticosum hirsutum*
 1 *Eupatorium purpureum*
 1 *Fuchsia* 'Riccartonii'
 3 *Geranium endressii* 'Wargrave Pink'
 3 *Geranium macrorrhizum*
16 *Iris germanica*
 2 *Juniperus virginiana* 'Skyrocket'
 1 *Kolkwitzia amabilis*
 7 *Lamium* 'Beacon Silver'
 1 *Nepeta mussinii* (catmint)
 1 *Paeonia* 'Bowl of Beauty'
 1 *Paeonia suffruticosa* 'Sakurajashi' (pink tree
       peony)
 1 *Prunus sargentii* (cherry tree)
 1 *Prunus subhirtella* 'Autumnalis' (cherry tree)
 2 *Rosa alba* 'Céleste'
 1 *Rosa* 'Altissimo'
 1 *Rosa* 'Constance Spry'
 2 *Rosa* 'Mme Isaac Pereire'
 1 *Rosa* 'Roseraie de l'Hay' (*rugosa*)
 1 *Rosa rubrifolia*
 1 *Rosa* 'The Fairy'
 1 *Rosa* 'White Wings'
 1 *Rosa* 'William Lobb' (moss)
 1 *Rosmarinus officinalis*
 6 *Salvia officinalis* 'Purpurascens' (purple sage)
 1 *Spiraea* 'Anthony Waterer'
 1 *Weigela* 'Newport Red'

Underplanting and summer bedding:
    Aquilegia (in variety)
    Leucanthemum vulgare (ox-eye daisy)
    Viola cornuta
    Wild strawberry

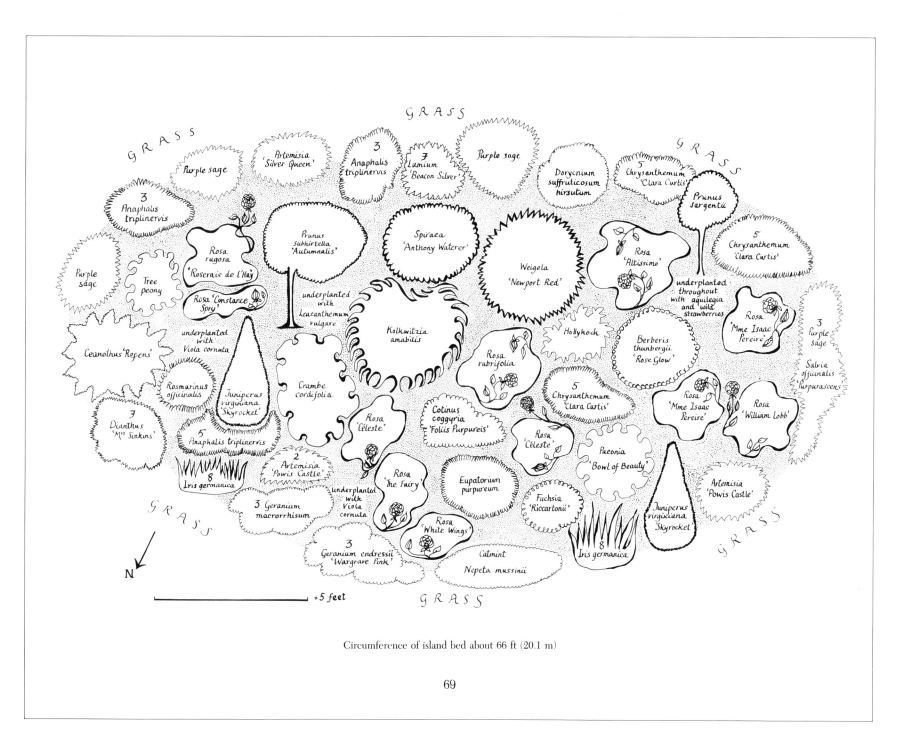

GRASS

GRASS

GRASS

Purple sage

Artemisia 'Silver Queen'

3 Anaphalis triplinervis

3 Lamium 'Beacon Silver'

Purple sage

Dorycnium suffruticosum hirsutum

5 Chrysanthemum 'Clara Curtis'

GRASS

3 Anaphalis triplinervis

Prunus sargentii

Purple sage

Tree peony

Rosa rugosa 'Roseraie de l'Hay'

Prunus subhirtella 'Autumnalis'

Spiraea 'Anthony Waterer'

Weigela 'Newport Red'

Rosa 'Altissimo'

5 Chrysanthemum 'Clara Curtis'

Rosa 'Constance Spry'

underplanted with Leucanthemum vulgare

underplanted throughout with aquilegia and wild strawberries

Ceanothus 'Repens'

underplanted with Viola cornuta

Kolkwitzia amabilis

Hollyhock

Berberis thunbergii 'Rose Glow'

Rosa 'Mme Isaac Pereire'

3 Purple sage

Rosmarinus officinalis

Juniperus virginiana 'Skyrocket'

Crambe cordifolia

Rosa rubrifolia

Salvia officinalis purpurascens

3 Dianthus 'Mrs Sinkins'

5 Anaphalis triplinervis

Rosa 'Céleste'

Cotinus coggygria 'Foliis Purpureis'

5 Chrysanthemum 'Clara Curtis'

Rosa 'Mme Isaac Pereire'

Rosa 'William Lobb'

Rosa 'Céleste'

8 Iris germanica

2 Artemisia 'Powis Castle'

Rosa 'The Fairy'

Eupatorium purpureum

Paeonia 'Bowl of Beauty'

Artemisia 'Powis Castle'

3 Geranium macrorrhizum

underplanted with Viola cornuta

Fuchsia 'Riccartonii'

Juniperus virginiana 'Skyrocket'

GRASS

3 Geranium endressii 'Wargrave Pink'

Rosa 'White Wings'

Catmint Nepeta mussinii

8 Iris germanica

GRASS

N

= 5 feet

GRASS

Circumference of island bed about 66 ft (20.1 m)

69

13

AN APRIL TO OCTOBER BORDER

The cry goes up these days for labour-saving gardens. This seems odd as acres dwindle and leisure expands, since it ought to be true that everybody who liked gardening would want more agreeable pottering with plants and less time spent with gadgets. Christopher Lloyd has no patience with people who regard everything as too much of a fiddle. He makes each inch of the famous long border at Dixter work overtime by using layers of plants, rather like John Sales in his garden (see Chapter 25), but unlike most other gardeners he also uses plenty of annuals and biennials. He likes change and can survive decay because it always provides a chance to grow something new. This combination of permanent fixtures and ephemera is not quite like any other. Most people who use annuals and summer bedding drop a few plants in near the front rather cautiously – Rosemary Verey is a little more daring and takes hers back in drifts – but Christopher Lloyd seems to change the whole look of a border just by cutting down or taking out one lot of plants and then substituting another.

In the section shown there is a permanent framework of colour and shape built round the golden elm. A variegated weigela and round-headed silver willow trees, which do well in the damp conditions of this clay-based garden, make a gentler contrast to golden leaves than the inevitable purple which appears in so many other plans in this book. There is some permanent purple from the berberis and rhus (which tend to languish on heavy, unimproved soil), but it is toned down by the grey of the willows. Evergreen is provided by the yew hedge and a mountain pine. All the trees and shrubs are controlled by pruning, which makes their leaves larger and keeps the plants in scale with the rest of the border. Shape is as important as colour and this comes in various forms: there are plumes of grass, spikes of yucca, feathered leaves of indigofera, and the architectural grandeurs of *Astilbe rivularis*, which is probably the best alternative to crambe for the gardener who works with heavy soil. Eryngium, artemisia, cannas, day lilies, chives and libertia all come in interesting shapes and there is really hardly anything in the border which looks dull when out of flower. Lilac is a classic example of a shrub with boring oval leaves, but here it is wreathed in Virginia creeper, so it ceases to matter what the leaves look like after the white flowers are over.

Like the Dixter border, plenty of types of planting illustrated in this book make strong statements, but very few have the strength, combined with the variety, which make this one so distinguished. There is a bold use of fleeting colour effects: brassy yellow and hot

OPPOSITE: *This famous gardener's border relies on annuals for a late-summer effect. Verbena bonariensis is self-seeding at Great Dixter.*

orange daisies, blood-red flowers of *Rosa moyesii* stalking near the edge of the bed, bright orange nasturtiums and the burnt-red of canna lilies, a combination of *Allium christophii* with *Sedum* 'Ruby Glow' and the red *Hydrangea* 'Preziosa' all put in an appearance in the same small section. There are whites, blues, pinks and mauves to take turns in toning down the hotter colours, but the effect is always clear and strong. The blue *Campanula persicifolia* runs wild everywhere and later in the year the old unimproved *Phlox paniculata*, in shades of mauve and white, appears throughout the planting. Both of these do well in heavy soils and would tend to disappear in less nourishing soil. In this bed the things which like good drainage are given plenty of grit, so that tender plants like salvias, verbenas and diascias do just as well as the heavy brigade. Bulbs like tulips and alliums also need to be planted in grit to survive the clay, and the proof that this works is furnished by their regular annual appearance at Dixter.

'Following through' is a Dixter dictum. Grape hyacinths are succeeded by pinky-orange alstroemerias, which then have their stems pulled out to make room for gentian-blue *Salvia patens*, the not so hardy tuberous salvia that rarely survives a winter. Nasturtiums take over from the foxtail lilies and clamber through the silvery artemisia. One

OPPOSITE: *Hydrangea* 'Preziosa' *has round, red flowers and is small enough to be included in most gardens. The lush, tropical leaves of canna lilies are a cool foil for hot-coloured flowers.*

year patches of ageratum and red flax might appear in the gaps around the indigofera; another season might bring something quite different. It is a fascinating mixture: old-fashioned plants like clematis and roses and the lanky Michaelmas daisies, which make a sea of misty blue, rub shoulders with bold foliage shrubs and interesting perennials, while simple annuals that any child could grow are allowed to climb all over the sort of plants which many people might despair of keeping.

Christopher Lloyd has worked for years at getting this border right yet he appears never to be satisfied. His gardening style is inimitable because it changes all the time. The things he tries are sometimes startling, but never safe, and he is much closer to the traditions of the artist gardeners, like Gertrude Jekyll and Russell Page, than those of the landscape gardeners. He claims that everything he does is unpremeditated, and emphasizes that being sensitive to a situation is what matters. He is, before all, a plantsman and likes the challenge of experiment, but what he has made reflects a broader view of gardening that creates a whole picture rather than just a collection of horticultural details.

LIST OF PLANTS

27 *Allium schoenoprasum* (giant chives)
7 *Anthemis sancti-johannis* (orange daisy)
3 *Artemisia lactiflora*
12 *Aster acris* (Michaelmas daisy)
3 *Aster ericoides* 'Esther'
3 *Astilbe rivularis*
1 *Berberis* × *ottawensis* 'Purpurea'
1 *Clematis* 'Gipsy Queen'

1 *Cotinus coggyria* 'Foliis purpureis'
5 *Eremurus robustus* (foxtail lilies)
3 *Eryngium* × *oliverianum*
2 *Geranium* 'Russell Prichard'
6 *Hydrangea* 'Lanarth White' (lacecap)
7 *Hydrangea* 'Preziosa'
1 *Indigofera kirilowi*
7 *Libertia peregrina* (from New Zealand, possible substitute *L. ixioides*)
1 *Miscanthus sinensis* 'Silver Feather' (giant grass)
1 *Parthenocissus inserta* (Virginia creeper)
1 *Pinus mugo* (mountain pine)
1 *Rosa* 'Chapeau de Napoléon'
2 *Rosa* 'Grüss an Aachen'
1 *Rosa moyesii*
3 *Salix alba* 'Argentea' (willow)
5 *Salvia nemorosa*
10 *Salvia patens* 'Cambridge Blue'
5 *Sedum* 'Ruby Glow'
1 *Syringa* 'Mme Lemoine' (lilac)
1 *Ulmus* × *sarniensis* 'Dicksonii' (golden elm)
6 *Viola cornuta* 'Alba'
1 *Yucca gloriosa* 'Variegata'

Underplanting and summer bedding:
Ageratum
Allium christophii
Allium ostrowskianum
Campanula persicifolia (blue)
Canna iridiflora (canna lilies)
Cuphea cyanea 'Firefly'
Diascia rigescens
Digitalis purpurea (foxglove, white or apricot)
Lathraea clandestina°
Linum rubrum (red flax)
Muscari in variety (grape hyacinth)
Myosotis sylvatica (forget-me-not)
Tropaeolum majus (nasturtium)
Nicotiana sylvestris
Tulipa 'Orange Favourite'
Verbena bonariensis
Viola odorata (violets planted under shrubs)

°A parasitic plant which only survives on the roots of willows.

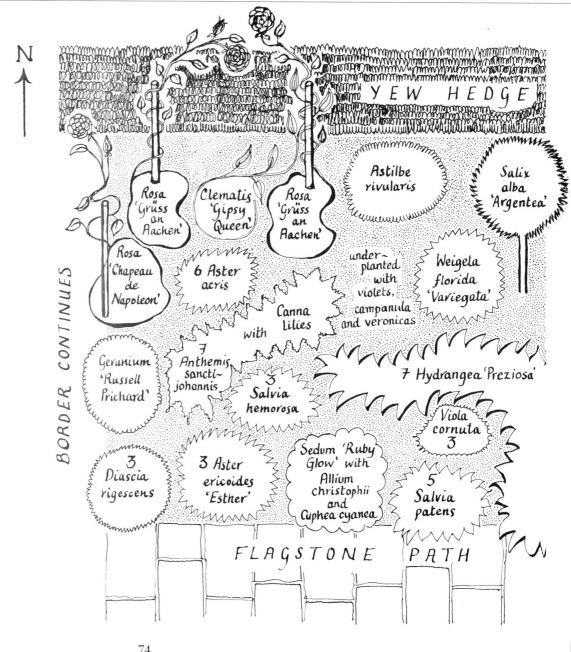

N

YEW HEDGE

Rosa 'Grüss an Aachen'

Clematis 'Gipsy Queen'

Rosa 'Grüss an Aachen'

Astilbe rivularis

Salix alba 'Argentea'

Rosa 'Chapeau de Napoleon'

6 Aster acris

under-planted with violets, campanula and veronicas

Weigela florida 'Variegata'

Canna Lilies with

Geranium 'Russell Prichard'

7 Anthemis sancti-johannis

3 Salvia hemorosa

7 Hydrangea 'Preziosa'

Viola cornuta 3

3 Diascia rigescens

3 Aster ericoides 'Esther'

Sedum 'Ruby Glow' with Allium christophii and Cuphea cyanea

5 Salvia patens

FLAGSTONE PATH

BORDER CONTINUES

DIMENSIONS: 45 × 15 ft (13.7 × 4.6 m)

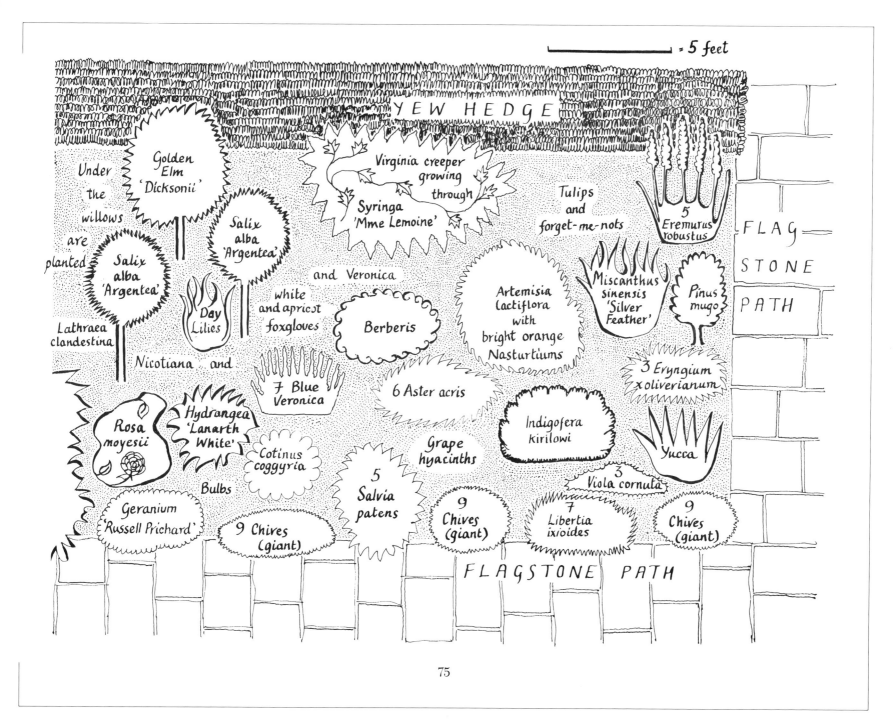

= 5 feet

YEW HEDGE

Golden Elm 'Dicksonii'

Under the willows are planted

Salix alba 'Argentea'

Salix alba 'Argentea'

Lathraea clandestina

Day Lilies

Nicotiana and

Virginia creeper growing through

Syringa 'Mme Lemoine'

Tulips and forget-me-nots

5 Eremurus robustus

FLAG STONE PATH

and Veronica

white and apricot foxgloves

Berberis

Artemisia lactiflora with bright orange Nasturtiums

Miscanthus sinensis 'Silver Feather'

Pinus mugo

7 Blue Veronica

6 Aster acris

3 Eryngium x oliverianum

Rosa moyesii

Hydrangea 'Lanarth White'

Cotinus coggyria

Grape hyacinths

Indigofera kirilowi

Yucca

Bulbs

Geranium 'Russell Prichard'

9 Chives (giant)

5 Salvia patens

9 Chives (giant)

3 Viola cornuta

7 Libertia ixioides

9 Chives (giant)

FLAGSTONE PATH

14

A HOT, DRY BANK WITH ARCHITECTURAL PLANTS

Fashions in gardening change just as much as they do in other matters of taste. Ten years ago, ground-cover plants for year-long interest were to be seen in the majority of gardens open to the public. Recently the mood has swung towards producing glorious effects for short periods, rather than aiming to furnish the gardens as a lasting, labour-saving background.

This hot, dry bank designed by a painter and his wife is a dramatic sight in June, and is found in a small garden which is currently one of the prettiest in the country. The group of cistuses and giant silver thistles set against a background of cloudy, white crambe is an unforgettable picture, made more theatrical by being planted on a bank which increases their already great height. On either side of the stone bench, bushes of a rare and very blue rosemary, grown from seed gathered in Cyprus, start the season by flowering in May. 'Benenden Blue' is easier and could be a substitute for this, but in less well-drained and favoured spots might have to be replaced by a hardier form like 'Blue Spire', which is not such a brilliant colour as either of the other two rosemaries. The blue theme is carried on by the towering bunches of anchusa, which flower in early summer. This plant is a bother to stake and is not long-lived in cold, heavy soils, but there is nothing to touch its azure, the colour of a Mediterranean sky. The hardiest of the cistuses chosen is *C. laurifolius*, but the other varieties planted here should present few problems in a warm garden on a sunny site, unless the winter proves exceptionally hard. The sisyrinchium ought to seed itself, or can be divided after flowering; in some gardens it will need encouragement, for it can disappear when grown on poor soil. When the cistus bushes finish flowering, the hardy *Geranium procurrens*, which has small purple flowers, extends the season by trailing over the shrubs in late summer. *Geranium wallichianum* 'Buxton's Blue' which blooms from July for four months and has white centres to its blue flowers would have been an equally good choice and some might prefer its soft colouring to the purple of *procurrens*.

The giant silver cotton thistle, onopordon, is a biennial which collapses shortly after flowering; carting it away is one of the most disagreeable tasks in the garden since it makes a cumbersome and prickly corpse. It is a daring plant to introduce in a small scale garden, because, at eight feet, it is so much larger than anything else, but for those who like the occasional surprise it introduces an element of drama. In this planting, the faint-hearted could probably replace it by the cardoon (*Cynara cardunculus*) which would not grow as tall, but I think this would be a pity. Crambe is another plant rarely recommended

OPPOSITE: *A cloud of crambe behind the giant silver thistle presents a bold picture in a small space.*

76

for small gardens. However, this patch of ground measuring fifteen feet by ten feet is a triumphant refutation to all who advocate caution and dwarf plants for homes which are less than stately.

Both the crambe and the onopordon do leave a gap when they are over; crambe's large green leaves continue to fill some space but can look rather tattered by the end of the summer. Here, the perennial gypsophila emerges in front of the crambes to make a smaller mass of white flowers, echoing the earlier cloudy effect of the larger plants. The gap left by the onopordons at the end of July is not filled by this owner, who feels that there are other places in the garden to come into their own once the early summer spectacle around the stone bench is over, so it does not matter if this area looks subdued for the rest of the year. A good plant to put in place of the onopordons, for those who wish to continue to enjoy that part of the garden, might be the giant tobacco plant, *Nicotiana sylvestris*, which can take any amount of drought and is even more heavily scented than the ordinary *Nicotiana affinis*. It would also be in scale with the rest of the planting.

An apple tree has recently been planted to replace one which died in the same corner, and this will ultimately change the character of the hot dry bank, even though the owners plan to keep it very open by hard pruning. It would be a mistake to include this tree if the

LEFT: *The cotton thistle provides an architectural feature at the end of a walk lined with iris and lavender.*

78

planting is to be a permanent fixture, because it would bring too much shade and a domestic feeling to what is at present a hot and exotic mood. Good gardens are rarely static and, like all committed gardeners, the owners of this one cannot resist the opportunity for a change; they regard this planting as a temporary effect which will be replaced by other plants that they long to grow. The thyme bank to the right of the group of giants has been lost in the course of a recent hard winter and new cistuses are to be planted in its place. These will form the nucleus for a different arrangement of shrubs and summer perennials, to make another fleeting image in the hot months of the year.

LIST OF PLANTS

1 *Anchusa* 'Loddon Royalist'
1 Apple tree 'Arthur Turner'
1 *Cistus* × *aguilari* 'Maculatus'
1 *Cistus* × *laurifolius*
1 *Cistus* × *corbariensis*
3 *Cistus* × *purpureus*
1 *Clematis* 'Jackmanii Superba'
3 *Crambe cordifolia*
1 *Deutzia monbeigii*
3 *Geranium collinum*
3 *Geranium procurrens*
4 *Gypsophila paniculata*
5 *Iris* 'Jane Phillips'
3 *Onopordon arabicum*
2 *Rosmarinus* 'Cypriot' (rosemary; possible sub-
    stitute 'Benenden Blue')
6 *Sisyrinchium striatum*
3 *Verbena rigida*

Underplanting and summer bedding:
    Foxgloves and lilies with a bank of common
    thyme.

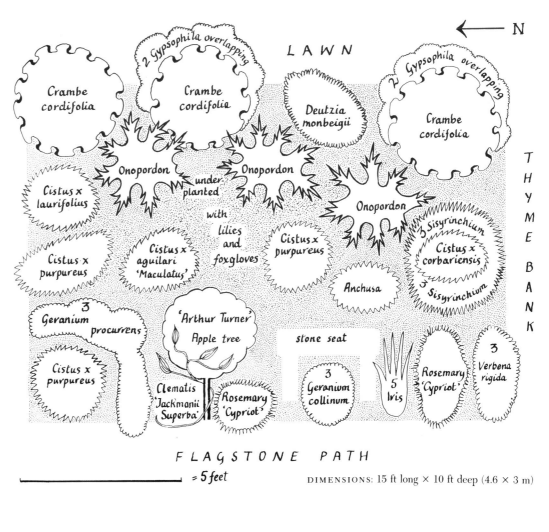

DIMENSIONS: 15 ft long × 10 ft deep (4.6 × 3 m)

15

A COURTYARD GARDEN

This courtyard in East Anglia forms part of a larger country garden, but the design could easily be used in a town since the dimensions are about the same as the average city plot. In narrower spaces it should still work, but the pool would need to be very much reduced. There is a pool at Hidcote which is no more than a sunken trough, situated in an area where yellow and orange plants are grouped. This would make a good model for a very small courtyard. Raised beds – here they are three bricks high – are always useful for accommodating extra soil in town gardens where conditions can be less than perfect, and they also provide the sharp drainage which many of the plants in this plan demand. Here the alkaline soil drains fast and rainfall is low, but the climate is not particularly kind. The courtyard provides shelter and ideal conditions for Mediterranean plants, and many town gardens could do the same.

The southern side of the garden is domin-ated by a black timbered barn with a cor-rugated roof, which is not a particularly easy background for plants, but the choice of pale coloured leaves all round the garden helps to reduce the impression of darkness. There are ivies everywhere on the west- and north-facing boundaries and many of them have variegated leaves. To balance the black barn clumps of yew stand against the opposite wall, so that everywhere the contrast between light and dark is strong. In winter, the view from the windows of the barn looks out onto green and white leaves, with the *Lonicera fragrantissima* growing on the warm wall, providing scented flowers all through the coldest months. There might be room somewhere among the ivies to put a *Jasminum nudiflorum*, which also flowers in winter, and snowdrops could grow along the northern bed. The conifers and house leeks in the pots around the pond provide some interest in winter. A few early bulbs are plan-ted in those pots along the edges of the border where the scented-leaf geraniums grow later in the year.

In hot months the courtyard becomes a place for sitting outside and the chairs are surrounded by plenty of scented plants. Cistuses have their foreign, resinous aroma, but the sweetbriar and jasmine smell of an English summer, while the *Clematis rehderana* breathes a faint hint of cowslips and all the leaves of the geraniums can be crushed in the hands of the passer-by. In town gardens, where traffic fumes coat the air, finding fragrant plants is a priority. Other kinds which might be included in a courtyard garden are lemon verbena (*Aloysia citriodora*), white tobacco plants, which could be grown in shade, the scented evening primrose (*Oenothera trichocalyx*) and the incense rose (*Rosa primula*).

OPPOSITE: *Pots of scented-leaf geraniums furnish the space at the centre of the small paved yard.*

Purple vines and blue salvias add hazy colour to a background of ivies and cistuses late in the year.

LIST OF PLANTS

NORTH-FACING WALL
1 *Clematis alpina* 'Frances Rivis'
1 *Clematis alpina* 'Willy'
1 *Clematis rehderana*
1 *Hedera colchica* 'Dentata Variegata' (ivy)
1 *Hedera helix canariensis* 'Glacier'
1 *Hedera hibernica* (Irish ivy)
1 *Jasminum officinale* 'Affine' (summer jasmine)
1 *Kerria japonica* 'Variegata'
1 *Parthenocissus henryana* (Virginia creeper)
1 *Rosa rubiginosa* (sweetbriar)
2 *Taxus baccata* (yew)

SOUTH-FACING WALL
1 *Abelia* × *grandiflora*
1 *Artemisia arborescens* 'Faith Raven'
1 *Ballota acetabulosa*
1 *Carpenteria californica*
1 *Ceanothus* 'Trewithen Blue'
1 *Clematis orientalis*
1 *Clematis texensis* 'Etoile Rose'
1 *Hebe* × *andersonii*
1 *Hebe armstrongii*
1 *Lonicera fragrantissima*
7 *Nerine bowdenii*
1 *Osteospermum ecklonis*
1 *Piptanthus laburnifolius*
1 *Rosa alexandra* (rare – possible substitute *Rosa primula*)
6 *Senecio leucostachys*
1 *Solanum jasminoides* 'Album'
1 *Sphaeralcea munroana*
1 *Teucrium chamaedrys* (germander)
1 *Teucrium fruticans*

WEST-FACING WALL
1 *Cistus* × *corbariensis*
2 *Cistus ladanifer*
1 *Clematis alpina* 'Ruby'
1 *Euphorbia dulcis*

In small areas there is no point in devoting space to plants which have a short flowering season and are dull for the rest of the year. Lilacs are a waste of time. Shrubs like the semi-evergreen piptanthus and the constantly flowering abelia are worth their place almost all the time. *Cyclamen hederifolium* remains attractive for over nine months of the year and their marbled leaves would look good under the north-wall border. There is scope, too, for growing carpets of thyme in the paving stones, but it would be a mistake to plant too much in the chinks of the paved area. In some of the cracks violets and ivy are already growing and any more plants would break the stillness of the courtyard.

1 *Hebe pagiana*
1 *Hedera canariensis* `Gloire de Marengo`
1 *Hedera colchica* 'Dentata Variegata'
1 *Hedera hibernica*
1 *Osteospermum* 'Buttermilk'
1 *Phygelius aequalis*
1 *Salvia guaranitica*
1 *Senecio leucostachys*
1 *Vitis* 'Brant'
1 *Wisteria sinensis* (Chinese wisteria)

Underplanting and summer bedding:
   Sphaeralcea munroana (under west-facing wall)
   Scented-leaf geranium (under north-facing
     wall)

In the pots:
   Conifers; house leeks; *Osteospermum ecklonis*
   (African daisies); scented-leaf geranium:
   Pelargonium tomentosum; *P. graveolens*; *P.
   crispum*

DIMENSIONS: 30 × 45 ft (9.1 × 13.7 m)

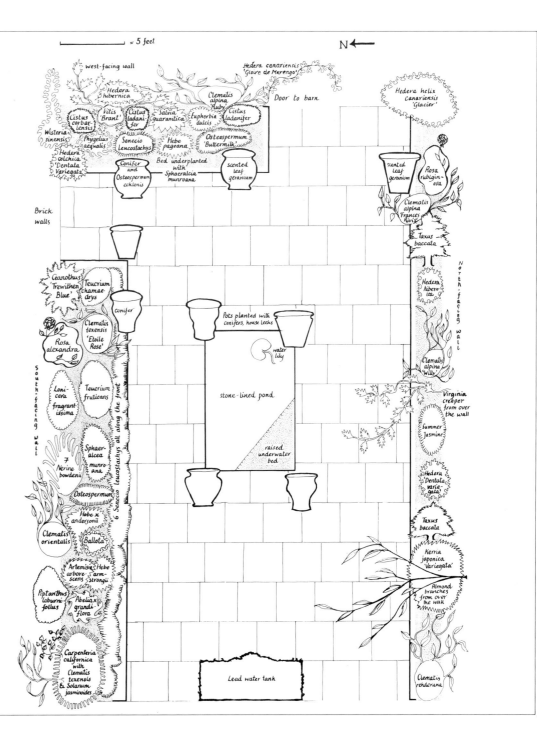

16

A FORMALLY LANDSCAPED BANK

In small gardens where there are no long views and the boundaries are always in evidence, a mounded bank with a four-foot retaining wall makes an unusual feature. Lanning Roper designed this circular arrangement to deal with a change of levels at the end of a gravel path in a Berkshire garden. Here a Regency birdcage tops a simple stone pool set in a retaining wall. This crowning folly was a happy find, but other architectural devices would serve almost as well. A castle of yew, or a stone cairn covered in ivy, or a not too sophisticated statue could all make a focal point, while a simple ironwork arbour painted white would have a similar effect to the birdcage. The planting is on quite a small scale and whatever is chosen for the top of the mound needs to be roughly twice as high as the retaining wall to keep the proportions in perspective.

This site was particularly damp and the fountain, which is not much more than a trickle of water over moss, was an attempt to channel the water and remedy the dampness. On dry banks, the wall could continue unbroken, or a curved seat might be introduced instead of the pool because it is very agreeable to sit at the edge of a circle surrounded by flowers, looking down a path lined with shady magnolias. None of the plants chosen should present any problems on a dry site, although the roses might need a mulch if the slope is very steep and the conditions poor. The varieties are all reliable. 'Comte de Chambord' is an old-fashioned rose with a much longer flowering season than most and deserves to be more widely planted. It is rich pink and many petalled, with a delicious smell.

'Charles de Mills' has a shorter flowering season and carries purple goblet-shaped flowers. 'Aloha' and 'The Alchemist' are two modern roses which never look out of place with the older sorts, but it may be time for a reappraisal of 'Iceberg'. This rose was the darling of the 1970s when no garden designer could resist a bush or two of the white floribunda which kept on flowering all summer. But the climbing form seen here does not flower as reliably as the shrub, and both sorts seem recently to have become very susceptible to black spot.

Hellebores, which hang their flowers, are seen at their best from below where their striped and freckled petals can be enjoyed without stooping. Since the planted area is so small it would be worth restricting the hellebores to the best forms for the patch at the front. Those plants at the back could be gradually improved by weeding out the dingy pink forms, until only the more interesting colours remained. In early spring these lenten

OPPOSITE: *The yellow flowers of senecio, seen against stone and in the company of ferns, are not to be despised, especially when toned down with splashes of white.*

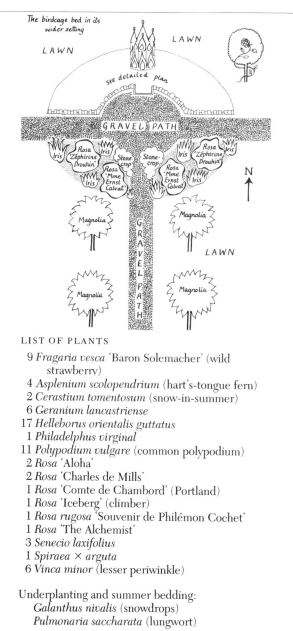

The birdcage bed in its wider setting

LAWN LAWN

see detailed plan

GRAVEL PATH

Iris · Rosa 'Zéphirine Drouhin' · Stonecrop · Stonecrop · Iris · Rosa 'Zéphirine Drouhin'

Rosa 'Mme Ernst Calvat' · Rosa 'Mme Ernst Calvat'

Iris · Iris

Magnolia · Magnolia

GRAVEL PATH

LAWN

Magnolia · Magnolia

N

LIST OF PLANTS

  9 *Fragaria vesca* 'Baron Solemacher' (wild strawberry)
  4 *Asplenium scolopendrium* (hart's-tongue fern)
  2 *Cerastium tomentosum* (snow-in-summer)
  6 *Geranium lancastriense*
17 *Helleborus orientalis guttatus*
  1 *Philadelphus virginal*
11 *Polypodium vulgare* (common polypodium)
  2 *Rosa* 'Aloha'
  2 *Rosa* 'Charles de Mills'
  1 *Rosa* 'Comte de Chambord' (Portland)
  1 *Rosa* 'Iceberg' (climber)
  1 *Rosa rugosa* 'Souvenir de Philémon Cochet'
  1 *Rosa* 'The Alchemist'
  3 *Senecio laxifolius*
  1 *Spiraea* × *arguta*
  6 *Vinca minor* (lesser periwinkle)

Underplanting and summer bedding:
  Galanthus nivalis (snowdrops)
  Pulmonaria saccharata (lungwort)

A miniature hanging garden completes the circle at the end of a gravelled path.

roses are out with the pulmonarias, following the snowdrops which are underplanted all over the bed. To introduce other bulbs besides the snowdrops might spoil the effect of coherence which Lanning Roper always advocated.

Ferns are generally associated with damp spots, but both the varieties chosen here are just as happy in dry places. These, and the wild strawberries, give the planting the feeling of a wilderness. In spite of its sophisticated layout, there is a feeling of the secret garden about it all; the outsize bushes of senecio, the trailing periwinkle and the great spill of snow-in-summer make it look like a ruined corner which has been abandoned to nature, and the contrived effect of an overgrown garden is very appealing. If the area was over-managed and tidied up it might all begin to look rather pretentious.

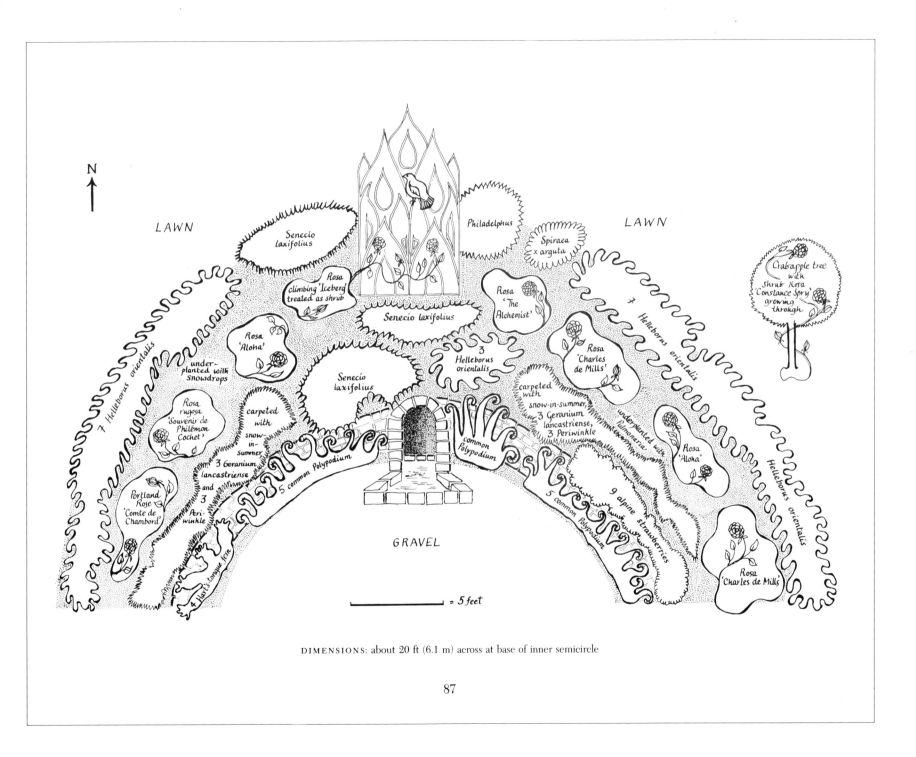

N

LAWN

LAWN

Senecio laxifolius

Philadelphus

Spiraea x arguta

Crabapple tree with Shrub Rosa 'Constance Spry' growing through

Rosa climbing 'Iceberg' treated as shrub

Rosa 'The Alchemist'

Senecio laxifolius

7 Helleborus orientalis

Rosa 'Aloha'

3 Helleborus orientalis

Rosa 'Charles de Mills'

7 Helleborus orientalis

underplanted with Snowdrops

Senecio laxifolius

carpeted with snow-in-summer, 3 Geranium lancastriense, 3 Periwinkle

Rosa rugosa 'Souvenir de Philémon Cochet'

carpeted with snow-in-summer

underplanted with Pulmonaria

Helleborus orientalis

3 Geranium lancastriense and 3 Periwinkle

common Polypodium

Rosa 'Aloha'

Portland Rose 'Comte de Chambord'

5 common Polypodium

9 alpine strawberries

4 Hart's-tongue fern

5 common Polypodium

GRAVEL

Rosa 'Charles de Mills'

= 5 feet

DIMENSIONS: about 20 ft (6.1 m) across at base of inner semicircle

87

17

A High-summer Border with Unusual Plants

This border is one of a pair of mirror beds, which repeat the same planting arrangement, and are part of a set of four in a Hampshire garden below the chalk Downs. They are herbaceous plantings which have been famous for over a quarter of a century, for they were made with a painter's eye. Their present owner, whose mother started the garden, describes them as pools of swirling colour in a wild cornucopia. The traditional plants are still there but the odd rarity has been added, making the borders an unusual display of horticultural interest combined with dramatic effect. People who are interested in rare plants tend to steer clear of bold groups and might easily sacrifice old favourites, like the lacquer-red oriental poppies at the back of the border, for something more special and probably less spectacular. Gardens which are just collections of treasures tend not to be as much fun for the casual visitor as gardens which are not so specialized. The best gardens of all, like this

one, have a mixture of the old with the new, as well as of the rare and the familiar. The main impact of the borders lasts from June to mid-July, although flowers start appearing earlier than this, with bushes of snow-white *Spiraea* × *arguta* and the delicate leaves of aquilegias and polemoniums carrying their flowers early in the year. Everything used to be finished by August but the aim recently has been to extend the season without diluting any of the high-summer glory. Plants like late-flowering asters and the giant yellow daisies of the inula keep the show going until well into the autumn and there are also annuals at the corners of the borders, quite ordinary ones like clary and *Echium* 'Blue Bedder', as well as plenty of pansies.

Most large borders are backed by a hedge or wall; it is always difficult to give a feeling of structure to a bed with little permanent anchorage. The straight lines do help to contain the planting but the large plants at the

core of the flowerbed are what really seem to hold everything firmly together. Crambe, with its foam of white flowers, and the giant silver thistle have appeared in other borders in this book, and the crambe school of gardening seems to be nearly as popular as the purple rhus and golden lonicera school. Some structure is always important and outsize herbaceous plants like the crambe and the giant thistle will always provide a rest for the eye, but they will not, of course, show up in winter to give the height and solidity that shrubs would give. In a border such as this, it would be a pity to coarsen the effect by including too many shrubs. The spiraeas are airy enough not to do so and can be used as hosts for later-flowering sweet peas, but any more might be too much.

OPPOSITE: *Bright, clear colours of magenta cranesbill, crimson poppies and blue delphiniums are a change from pastel shades.*

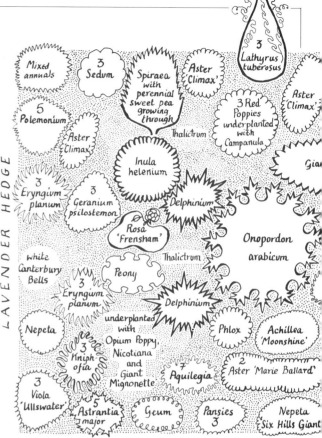

Plant bed diagram labels:

Mixed annuals · 3 *Sedum* · *Spiraea with perennial sweet pea growing through* · *Aster 'Climax'* · 3 *Lathyrus tuberosus* · *Aster 'Climax'* · 5 *Polemonium* · *Aster 'Climax'* · *Thalictrum* · 3 Red Poppies underplanted with *Campanula* · Gia... · *Inula helenium* · 3 *Eryngium planum* · 3 *Geranium psilostemon* · *Delphinium* · *Rosa 'Frensham'* · *Onopordon arabicum* · white Canterbury Bells · *Thalictrum* · *Peony* · 3 *Eryngium planum* · *Delphinium* · *Nepeta* · underplanted with Opium Poppy, *Nicotiana* and Giant Mignonette · *Phlox* · *Achillea 'Moonshine'* · 3 *Kniphofia* · 7 *Aquilegia* · 2 *Aster 'Marie Ballard'* · 3 *Viola 'Ullswater'* · *Astrantia major* · *Geum* · Pansies 3 · *Nepeta 'Six Hills Giant'*

LAVENDER HEDGE

Grand borders which are not backed by anything are hard to plant. Structure here comes from using repeated clumps of large plants along the whole length of the bed.

The other dominating presences in the bed early in the year are the clumps of brilliant blue comfrey. The bright pink pea (*Lathyrus tuberosus*) twines into a birdcage of peasticks which are placed at regular intervals along the back of the border. At the end of the summer, swags of the big, yellow daisy (inula) appear, so that there is always something on the grand scale to look at. The colours start as blue, with flashes of red, and gradually change to yellow.

All the plants are in rather smaller groups than is usual for such a large bed. This gives a kaleidoscopic effect, but it can be difficult to manage as there is a danger that the bed will end up looking spotty – although it never does

here. Nothing had been split for nineteen years until very recently, when all the borders were emptied and replanted. The aim now is to lift and divide plants every three years, with the exception of things like the peonies which prefer to be left alone. Few of the plants should present difficulties, but some might be hard to find. The border clematis obviously enjoys the chalk, roses do not. The only rose in the bed is the old dark red 'Frensham', which generally has gone out of favour since it has become so prone to mildew. It might be better to change this; in a warm place 'Cramoisie Supérieur', which is a long-flowering crimson china rose, would make a lovely alternative.

LIST OF PLANTS

6 *Achillea* 'Moonshine'
14 *Aquilegia alpina* (white or purple columbine)
5 *Aster* 'Climax' (blue Michaelmas daisy)
2 *Aster* 'Marie Ballard'
10 *Astrantia major*
2 *Baptisia australis* (yellow form)
15 *Campanula lactiflora*
5 *Campanula medium* (white Canterbury bell)
20 *Campanula persicifolia* (blue or white)
1 *Clematis × durandii*
2 *Clematis × eriostemon* 'Hendersonii'
1 *Crambe cordifolia*

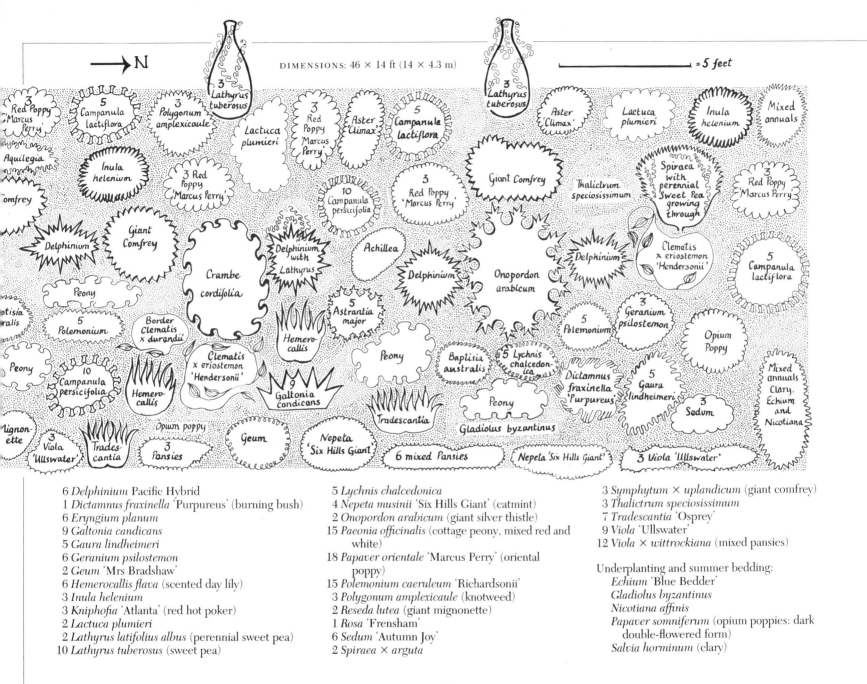

6 *Delphinium* Pacific Hybrid
1 *Dictamnus fraxinella* 'Purpureus' (burning bush)
6 *Eryngium planum*
9 *Galtonia candicans*
5 *Gaura lindheimeri*
6 *Geranium psilostemon*
2 *Geum* 'Mrs Bradshaw'
6 *Hemerocallis flava* (scented day lily)
3 *Inula helenium*
3 *Kniphofia* 'Atlanta' (red hot poker)
2 *Lactuca plumieri*
2 *Lathyrus latifolius albus* (perennial sweet pea)
10 *Lathyrus tuberosus* (sweet pea)

5 *Lychnis chalcedonica*
4 *Nepeta musinii* 'Six Hills Giant' (catmint)
2 *Onopordon arabicum* (giant silver thistle)
15 *Paeonia officinalis* (cottage peony, mixed red and
   white)
18 *Papaver orientale* 'Marcus Perry' (oriental
   poppy)
15 *Polemonium caeruleum* 'Richardsonii'
3 *Polygonum amplexicaule* (knotweed)
2 *Reseda lutea* (giant mignonette)
1 *Rosa* 'Frensham'
6 *Sedum* 'Autumn Joy'
2 *Spiraea* × *arguta*

3 *Symphytum* × *uplandicum* (giant comfrey)
3 *Thalictrum speciosissimum*
7 *Tradescantia* 'Osprey'
9 *Viola* 'Ullswater'
12 *Viola* × *wittrockiana* (mixed pansies)

Underplanting and summer bedding:
   Echium 'Blue Bedder'
   Gladiolus byzantinus
   Nicotiana affinis
   Papaver somniferum (opium poppies: dark
      double-flowered form)
   Salvia horminum (clary)

18

AUTUMN COLOUR IN A GRAVELLED GARDEN

Autumn colour is better left out of small gardens where the scale is wrong for seasonal grand effects which leave large areas of dullness for the rest of the year. This planting is a clever arrangement which gives an illusion of autumn colours; on examination it turns out to be trees and shrubs with a few perennials, which look respectable for most of the year. Most of its later colour comes not from leaves, but from berries which last much longer than the flash of brilliance as the first frosts touch the trees. Fruit and berries suggest autumn and harvest festival, and go on suggesting them almost until Christmas. Permanent leaf colour from golden- and red-leafed shrubs, together with the late spikes of red and yellow pokers, produce the same sort of tones that we expect to see in autumn, but take up less room than stands of beeches and cherry trees in the English countryside, or the nyssas at Sheffield Park. These are all a wonderful sight, but their impact cannot be scaled down for everyday use.

The question of using yellow and purple as complementary colours, which crops up in this border, is very vexed. Although they are complements in the colour spectrum, many people (including this author) find their juxtaposition brash and over-dramatic. Landscape architects and garden designers seem to love it: see Peter Coats's border in Chapter 2, John Brookes's in Chapter 8, and Graham Stuart Thomas's design for The National Trust in Chapter 28, all of which use this colour scheme in varying degrees. The combination seems to me to be tolerable when one of the colours is not at full strength, or when the plants are parted by something else which could tone down the clash of Titans. I find purple rhus next to golden lonicera unacceptably brash; pale yellow, or better still, cream, is easier on the eye than butter-yellow surrounded by purple. This is obviously a matter of taste, but as yellow and purple have appeared in so many borders in this book, and

there may be others who share a preference for more subdued associations, it is a problem worth considering. Those who cannot face the direct confrontation of purple and gold should think about changing one of the plants for something paler. Here it would be easy to substitute the cotinus from the purple to the green form (which colours beautifully in autumn), or perhaps to replace the lonicera with another *rubrifolia* rose.

Some minor adjustments to colour could also be made by rearranging reds and yellows. The crab apples of *Malus × robusta* are scarlet; there is a yellow form, but if this were used there might then be too much yellow in the bed. The *Viburnum opulus* is the familiar guelder rose whose leaves colour well in

OPPOSITE: *In gardens which are too small for a range of trees autumn colour can be suggested by using yellow and orange herbaceous plants. Red hot pokers and crab apples look like harvest festival time.*

Malus robusta has clusters of red apples which hang until Christmas.

autumn and, in this form, has yellow rather than red fruit. Those who prefer yellow to red could change the crab to yellow and the viburnum to red, thus maintaining the balance of colour, but with a different emphasis. It is important to remember that the guelder rose does not produce berries on the sterile 'Snowball' form, which is often the only available variety at garden centres. This version of the shrub has round, white balls of flowers in June, while the native of hedgerows on chalky soils which does produce the berries has flat, white flowers, more like a cross between an elder and a lacecap hydrangea. The best form of the non-sterile variety is 'Compactum'. The variegated snowberry, which has pinkish berries, is better planted in sun, because it can lose its variegation when grown in the shade.

The hogweed is a spectacular biennial, which should renew itself from year to year, but it can become invasive. The other disadvantage is that some people are allergic to this plant and will develop an uncomfortable rash. Angelica might be a possible substitute here.

The layer of gravel which surrounds the shrubs makes for very easy maintenance and provides a cooling mulch in summer. Any weeds that do grow can easily be eliminated and a deep layer of gravel always improves the drainage in a bed. This can be a help where the hardiness of plants is doubtful; in this case it is not a problem, apart from the red hot pokers which might give trouble in colder zones.

LIST OF PLANTS

9 *Anthemis cupaniana*
3 *Aralia elata* (Japanese angelica tree)
1 *Berberis thunbergii* 'Atropurpurea'
1 *Bupleurum fruticosum*
1 *Buxus latifolia maculata* (golden box)
1 *Choisya ternata*
1 *Cotinus coggyria*
1 *Cotoneaster horizontalis* 'Variegatus'
1 *Elaeagnus* × *ebbingei*
4 *Euphorbia robbiae*
2 *Hedera* 'Glymii' (ivy)
1 *Heracleum mantegazzianum* (hogweed)
1 *Kniphofia* 'Corallina' (red hot poker: coral; or for an alternative: 'Underway')
9 *Kniphofia* 'Royal Standard' (red hot poker)
1 *Lonicera nitida* 'Baggesen's Gold'
5 *Lysimachia nummularia* (creeping jenny)
1 *Malus robusta* (crab apple)
9 *Mentha rotundifolia* 'Variegata' (apple mint)
1 *Phlomis russeliana*
1 *Rosa rubrifolia*
1 *Rosmarinus officinalis* 'Miss Jessup's Upright'
3 *Salvia* 'Icterina' (golden sage)
1 *Senecio laxifolius*
1 *Sorbus aria* 'Lutescens' (whitebeam)
1 *Spiraea* × *bumalda* 'Goldflame'
3 *Symphoricarpos orbiculatus* 'Variegatus' (snowberry)
1 *Viburnum opulus* 'Xanthocarpum' (guelder rose)
1 *Viburnum tinus* (laurustinus)
5 *Vinca major* 'Variegata' (periwinkle)

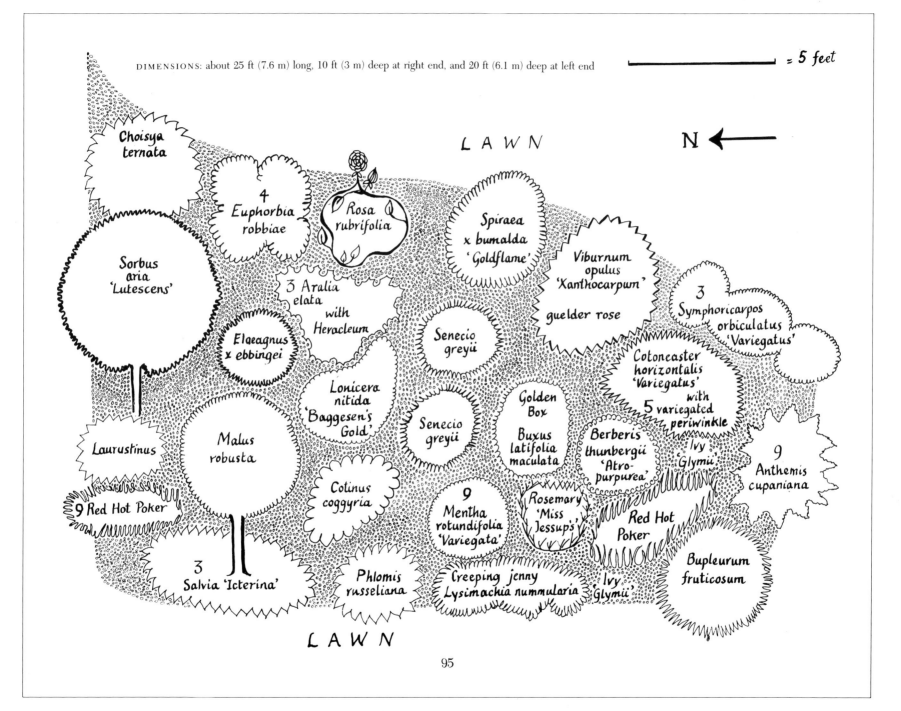

DIMENSIONS: about 25 ft (7.6 m) long, 10 ft (3 m) deep at right end, and 20 ft (6.1 m) deep at left end

= 5 feet

L A W N

N

Choisya
ternata

4
Euphorbia
robbiae

Rosa
rubrifolia

Spiraea
x bumalda
'Goldflame'

Viburnum
opulus
'Xanthocarpum'

guelder rose

3
Symphoricarpos
orbiculatus
'Variegatus'

Sorbus
aria
'Lutescens'

3 Aralia
elata

with
Heracleum

Senecio
greyii

Cotoneaster
horizontalis
'Variegatus'

Elaeagnus
x ebbingei

Lonicera
nitida
'Baggesen's
Gold'

Senecio
greyii

Golden
Box

5 with
variegated
periwinkle

Laurustinus

Malus
robusta

Buxus
latifolia
maculata

Berberis
thunbergii
'Atro-
purpurea'

Ivy
'Glymii'

9
Anthemis
cupaniana

Cotinus
coggyria

9 Red Hot Poker

9
Mentha
rotundifolia
'Variegata'

Rosemary
'Miss
Jessup's'

Red Hot
Poker

3
Salvia 'Icterina'

Phlomis
russeliana

Creeping jenny
Lysimachia nummularia

Ivy
'Glymii'

Bupleurum
fruticosum

L A W N

95

19

A TRIANGULAR BED

Russell Page (1906–85) was one of the great English landscape architects of this century. He was a painter who studied at the Slade and in Paris and who then turned to gardening in the manner of Gertrude Jekyll. His book, *The Education of a Gardener*, is an inspiration to all gardeners who are interested in more than just horticulture and the gardens he made were faultless and enviable. The Culpeper Garden at Leeds Castle was one of his last commissions before he died. The layout of the beds and the spirit of the flowery enclosure is his, but most of the subsequent planting has been carried out by Stephen Crisp, the present gardener at Leeds. The beds were always meant to be full of traditional flowers – shrub roses, peonies, lilies and irises often featured in Russell Page's plantings – but he was particularly strong on the shapes and forms of leaves and liked to look at a planting as an exercise in monochrome, 'to see form only and let the colour ride'. He disliked classic herbaceous borders and described them as 'extensive and brightly flowered hay which has neither body nor character enough to make broad planting look other than flimsy'. He generally chose to use colour in varying harmonies and preferred the occasional accent of contrasting colour to a stronger clash.

The sort of plants which he used for texture in a planting were hostas, bergenias, ferns, grasses and silver-leafed plants. Those which he used for structure were often shrubs like *Buddleia alternifolia* (he disliked other forms), *Spartium junceum*, *Berberis thunbergii* (but never as a foil for yellow) and *Hydrangea paniculata* 'Grandiflora'. For dark spots in a planting he might have added clipped box or yew, or perhaps a pine like the *Pinus mugo* in the Red Border at Hidcote, which was the garden that he claimed had most influenced him. Finally the whole composition of Russell Page's planting had to blend in with the landscape, so that whatever was chosen was appropriate for the setting.

Such high standards are hard to follow but Stephen Crisp has made his own contribution to Russell Page's design. Because the garden is open to the public, who expect a continuous display of colour in the flowerbeds, the main aim has been to provide broad splashes of colour, but to include the rare and unusual plants which Stephen Crisp likes to grow. The national collections of monarda (bergamot) and nepeta (catmint) are kept at Leeds so there are plenty of varieties of both these families. There is a little of Russell Page in some of the arrangements of the plants: the purple-leaved weigela makes a dusky foil to pink, violet and crimson flowers; the grasses, acanthus and silver-leaved plants provide some variety of texture (although not, perhaps, as

OPPOSITE: *Hedges of box surround large plants in scale with the distant view.*

Verbena bonariensis is six feet tall but never dense. The occasional one at the front of a border makes a surprising change of height.

LIST OF PLANTS

1 *Acanthus spinosus*
7 *Allium giganteum*
7 *Anemone japonica*
1 *Artemisia schmidtiana* 'Nana'
1 *Aster amellus* 'Nocturne'
3 *Avena candida*
1 *Buddleia* 'Empire Beauty'
1 *Clerodendrum trichotomum*
3 *Dianthus* 'Widdicombe Fair' (pinks)
1 *Erigeron glaucus*
3 *Eryngium alpinum*
1 *Euphorbia dulcis*
1 *Fuchsia* 'Army Nurse'
1 *Fuchsia magellanica* 'Versicolor'
3 *Geranium sanguineum lancastriense*
1 *Helichrysum angustifolium* (curry plant)
1 *Helichrysum macrophyllum*
7 *Iris pallida Dalmatica*
1 *Lamium maculatum* 'Roseum'
1 *Lasiogrostis splendens* (large grass)
1 *Lavandula* 'Loddon Pink'
1 *Limonium sinuatum* (sea lavender)
6 *Lupinus* 'Russell hybrids' (lupins)
1 *Lythrum salicaria* 'Robert' (purple loosestrife)
1 *Malva alcea* 'Fastigiata'
3 *Monarda* 'Prairie Night' (bergamot)
1 *Nepeta* 'Blue Beauty'
1 *Nepeta mussinii* 'Improved' (catmint)
2 *Nepeta* 'Valerie Finnis' (possible substitute *N. × faassenii*)
1 *Panicum virgatum* 'Rubrum'
1 *Penstemon* 'Apple Blossom'
3 *Polygonum campanulatum*
1 *Pulmonaria officinalis*
1 *Rosa* 'F. J. Grootendorst'
1 *Rosa moyesii*
2 *Rosa rubrifolia*
2 *Rosa* 'Tuscany'
9 *Silene maritima* 'Rosea' (sea campion)
3 *Teucrium chamaedrys*
7 *Verbena bonariensis*

much as Page might have included had the design been exclusively his own) and there are no garish colour contrasts between the flowers. Flowering shrubs are included to give some solidity to the 'brightly flowered hay'. The invaluable guelder rose and the clerodendrum both have strong leaves and the pink 'F. J. Grootendorst' rose is of the *rugosa* type which Russell Page liked to include in all his gardens, although the *rugosa* he used most was 'Blanc Double de Coubert' rather than the one chosen here.

There is a good spread of interest from Easter to the end of October, and bedding plants such as the pink mallow (*Lavatera* 'Silver Cup') and nicotiana are used to cover up for things like lupins, which have a dis-agreeable way of dying. The border would work well in the corner of a small garden, furnished with shades of pinks, reds and mauves for most of the year. The verbenas would have to be treated as half-hardy annu-als in cold places, but otherwise there is not much to cause trouble in the average garden. The low hedge of box which surrounds the bed means that there is a frame of green to look at all winter, but in gardens where this was the only flowerbed it might be a good idea to include another evergreen in the middle of the bed to keep something else in the picture. *Laurustinus* 'Eve Price', or one of the other dark shrubs which Russell Page so often chose, could replace the clerodendrum without too much damage to the summer show.

3 *Verbena rigida*
1 *Viburnum opulus* 'Compactum'
1 *Weigela florida* 'Foliis Purpureis'

Underplanting and summer bedding:
  Allium roseum
  Aquilegia 'McKana Hybrids' (columbines)
  Lavatera 'Silver Cup' (pink mallow)

Lunaria annua (honesty)
Lupinus 'Russell Hybrids'
Nepeta mussinii 'Improved'
Nicotiana affinis 'Lime Green'
Papaver somniferum (opium poppies)
Tulipa clusiana chrysantha
Tulipa praestans 'Fusilier'
Tulipa turkestanica
Verbena rigida

= 5 feet

N ←

DIMENSIONS: similar to an equilateral triangle of roughly 33 ft (10 m) each side

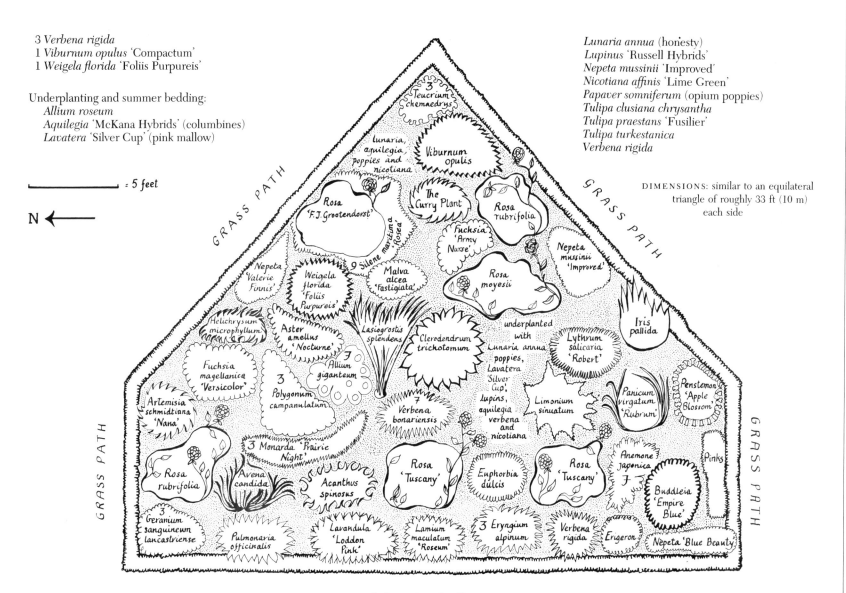

GRASS PATH

GRASS PATH

GRASS PATH

GRASS PATH

GRASS PATH

3 Teucrium chamaedrys

lunaria, aquilegia, poppies and nicotiana

Viburnum opulis

Rosa 'F.J. Grootendorst'

The Curry Plant

Rosa rubrifolia

Fuchsia 'Army Nurse'

Nepeta 'Valerie Finnis'

Weigela florida 'Foliis Purpureis'

9 Silene maritima 'Rosea'

Malva alcea 'Fastigiata'

Rosa moyesii

Nepeta mussinii 'Improved'

Helichrysum microphyllum

Aster amellus 'Nocturne'

Lasiogrostis splendens

Clerodendrum trichotomum

underplanted with Lunaria annua poppies, Lavatera 'Silver Cup', lupins, aquilegia verbena and nicotiana

Iris pallida

Lythrum salicaria 'Robert'

Fuchsia magellanica 'Versicolor'

3 Polygonum campanulatum

7 Allium giganteum

7 Verbena bonariensis

Limonium sinuatum

Panicum virgatum 'Rubrum'

Penstemon 'Apple Blossom'

Artemisia schmidtiana 'Nana'

Rosa rubrifolia

3 Monarda 'Prairie Night'

Avena candida

Acanthus spinosus

Rosa 'Tuscany'

Euphorbia dulcis

Rosa 'Tuscany'

Anemone 3 japonica

Pinks

Buddleia 'Empire Blue'

3 Geranium sanguineum lancastriense

Pulmonaria officinalis

Lavandula 'Loddon Pink'

Lamium maculatum 'Roseum'

3 Eryngium alpinum

Verbena rigida

Erigeron

Nepeta 'Blue Beauty'

GRASS PATH

99

20

A SMALL SHRUB ROSE BORDER

Clever use of space in this corner of a small garden creates an intriguing effect on a tiny scale. Shrub roses and topiary are usually thought of as elements in a grand design, but here they are reduced to sizes which could be accommodated in almost any garden. In spring the narrow double borders in front of the Cotswold stone wall are pale gold with flashes of pink; in summer they are a tapestry of rich colour. During a good winter all the cheiranthus is evergreen, or grey, which helps to furnish the garden. However, these plants are not reliable and, because this is a cold garden, there is a fairly rapid turnover of the less hardy plants, such as the perennial wall-flowers and the diascias, which provide dependable colour for many months. This does not matter too much as the plants deteriorate after a couple of years and need to be renewed anyway, which is easily done from cuttings. 'Bowles Mauve' is one of the best varieties of cheiranthus for a small garden because it flowers throughout spring and into early July, when it is worth cutting the bush back hard so that it flowers again in autumn. While the cheiranthus rest, the diascias take over and in most years there are osteo-spermums pushed into every available gap which will, like the diascias, flower all summer. White petunias and tobacco plants are also included, and somehow there is room for all these plants in the patches where the tulips have been as well as in other places. All of these go on flowering until the autumn frosts.

Perhaps the cleverest feature of this very economical use of space is the treatment of the roses. Shrub roses are usually seen blowing about in huge bushes in gardens where there is plenty of room for their untidy habits. *Rosa* 'Complicata' (gallica) can make a bush ten feet wide and almost as high, for it is a vigorous grower if left unpruned. In this garden it is kept severely in order and the flowers do not suffer at all. 'Fantin Latour' is another large shrub rose which is not normally pruned, but here it is grown in reduced form and, if anything, the flowers produced are even better than the ones which grow on untutored bushes. Another way of treating large shrub roses in small spaces is to peg them down to arches of hazel, but here the effect that is needed is vertical so many of the roses are grown as standards. The domed bushes which result from pegging down would occupy too much precious room. *Rosa* 'de Resht', an uncommon choice but a very good one, is a neat rose producing small double crimson flowers throughout the summer. It was a favourite of Nancy Lindsay's, an influential gardener who collected it in Persia. 'Petite de Hollande' is another good choice for a small garden. For those who long to grow

OPPOSITE: *Shrub roses can be grown as standards and pruned to fit small quarters. A variegated holly tree on the lawn grows in a square of golden marjoram.*

old-fashioned roses a possibility might be centifolia 'de Meaux' which flowers earlier than 'Petite de Hollande', but it would be hard to better the selection made here. 'The Fairy' (grown as a standard) takes care of the late summer from the middle of July until the autumn. In a paler colour scheme 'Little White Pet' could take its place, but it would be a pity to diminish the glowing colours of this planting which makes such a rich display in so small an area. Eleven feet by twenty-two feet makes a good sized room, but in a garden it is not a lot of space.

An ingenious design with a good structure has made the most of what is available, and an impeccable selection of plants which will give good value for a long time has resulted in a *tour de force*.

Alliums and roses make good companions. There is a school of thought which believes that garlic keeps the greenfly at bay.

LIST OF PLANTS

2 *Abutilon suntense*
1 *Actinidia chinensis* (kiwi fruit)
1 *Alyssum saxatile*
7 *Aquilegia vulgaris* (white columbines)
1 *Artemisia* 'Powis Castle'
1 *Astrantia* 'Variegata'
1 *Bergenia stracheyi* 'Alba'
12 *Buxus* 'Suffruticosa' (box hedge)
3 *Campanula latiloba* 'Alba'
1 *Cardamine pratensis* 'Flore Pleno' (double lady's smock)
1 *Ceanothus* × 'Autumnal Blue'
3 *Cheiranthus* 'Bowles Mauve' (perennial wallflower)
2 *Cheiranthus* 'Harpur Crewe' (perennial wallflower)
2 *Cheiranthus* 'Wenlock Beauty' (perennial wallflower)
1 *Cistus laurifolius*
1 *Cistus* 'Silver Pink'
1 *Clematis* 'Beauty of Worcester'
1 *Clematis* × *durandii*
1 *Clematis* 'Etoile Rose'
1 *Clematis* × 'Jackmanii Superba'
1 *Clematis* 'Rubra'
1 *Cytisus battandieri*
1 *Cytisus* × *praecox*
1 *Diascia rigescens*
1 *Dicentra spectabilis* 'Alba'
1 *Euphorbia polychroma*
1 *Foeniculum vulgare purpureum* (purple fennel)
1 *Geranium* 'Claridge Druce' (cranesbill)
1 *Geranium* 'Johnson's Blue' (cranesbill)
1 *Geranium macrorrhizum* (cranesbill)
1 *Geranium sanguineum* 'Album' (cranesbill)
1 *Helichrysum angustifolium* (curry plant)
4 *Hosta* 'Albomarginata'
1 *Hosta sieboldiana*
1 *Juniperus* 'Pfitzerana'
1 *Juniperus* 'Skyrocket'
1 *Lonicera* 'Serotina'
1 *Lonicera syringantha*

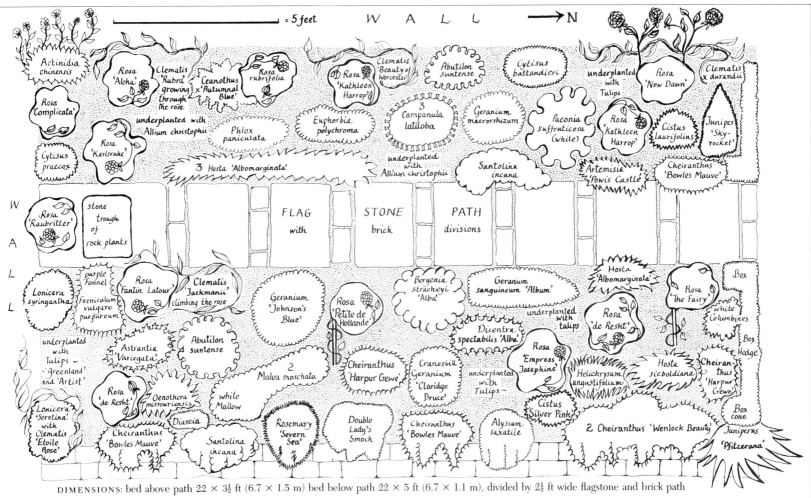

= 5 feet   W A L L   → N

Actinidia chinensis

Rosa 'Aloha'
Clematis 'Rubri' growing through the rose
Ceanothus x 'Autumnal Blue'
Rosa rubrifolia
Rosa 'Kathleen Harrop'
Clematis 'Beauty of Worcester'
Abutilon suntense
Cytisus battandieri
underplanted with Tulips
Rosa 'New Dawn'
Clematis x durandii

Rosa 'Complicata'
underplanted with Allium christophii
Phlox paniculata
Euphorbia polychroma
3 Campanula latiloba
Geranium macrorrhizum
Paeonia suffruticosa (white)
Rosa 'Kathleen Harrop'
Cistus laurifolius
Juniper 'Skyrocket'

Cytisus praecox
Rosa 'Karlsruhe'
3 Hosta 'Albomarginata'
underplanted with Allium christophii
Santolina incana
Artemisia 'Powis Castle'
Cheiranthus 'Bowles Mauve'

W A L L

Rosa 'Raubritter'
stone trough of rock plants
FLAG   STONE   PATH
with   brick   divisions

purple fennel
Lonicera syringantha
Foeniculum vulgare purpureum
Rosa 'Fantin Latour'
Clematis 'Jackmanii' climbing the rose
Geranium 'Johnson's Blue'
Rosa 'Petite de Hollande'
Bergenia stracheyi 'Alba'
Geranium sanguineum 'Album'
Hosta 'Albomarginata'
Rosa 'The Fairy'
Box
white Columbines
Box Hedge

underplanted with Tulips – 'Greenland' and 'Artist'
Astrantia 'Variegata'
Abutilon suntense
2 Malva moschata
Cheiranthus 'Harpur Crewe'
Cranesbill Geranium 'Claridge Druce'
Dicentra spectabilis 'Alba'
underplanted with Tulips –
Rosa 'Empress Josephine'
Rosa 'de Resht'
Helichrysum angustifolium
Hosta sieboldiana
Cheiranthus 'Harpur Crewe'

Lonicera 'Serotina' with Clematis 'Etoile Rose'
Rosa 'de Resht'
Oenothera missouriensis
white Mallow
Diascia
Santolina incana
Rosemary 'Severn Sea'
Double Lady's Smock
Cheiranthus 'Bowles Mauve'
Alyssum saxatile
Cistus 'Silver Pink'
2 Cheiranthus 'Wenlock Beauty'
Box cone
Cheiranthus 'Bowles Mauve'
Juniperus 'Pfitzerana'

DIMENSIONS: bed above path 22 × 3½ ft (6.7 × 1.5 m) bed below path 22 × 5 ft (6.7 × 1.1 m), divided by 2½ ft wide flagstone and brick path

2 *Malva moschata* (white mallow)
1 *Oenothera missouriensis* (evening primrose)
1 *Paeonia suffruticosa* (white)
1 *Phlox paniculata*
1 *Rosa* 'Aloha'
1 *Rosa* 'Complicata'
2 *Rosa* 'de Resht'
1 *Rosa* 'Empress Josephine'
1 *Rosa* 'Fantin Latour'

1 *Rosa* 'Karlsruhe'
2 *Rosa* 'Kathleen Harrop'
1 *Rosa* 'New Dawn'
1 *Rosa* 'Petite de Hollande'
1 *Rosa* 'Raubritter'
1 *Rosa* rubrifolia
1 *Rosa* 'The Fairy' (standard)
1 *Rosmarinus* 'Severn Sea'
2 *Santolina incana*

Underplanting and summer bedding:
   Allium christophii
   Nicotiana affinis (tobacco plant)
   Osteospermum ecklonis
   Petunia hybrida (white petunias)
   Tulipa 'Artist' and 'Greenland'

103

Leaf Forms and Shades of Green for Spring

Visitors to large traditional gardens often feel dispirited when they see double herbaceous borders backed by mature trees and set in rolling lawns. The scale of everything seems too big to adapt to anything at home and so they stop looking at the plants and gaze enviously at the general effect. This chapter's planting forms the end to one side of just such a double border. Both of the beds are packed with distinguished plants, and from a seat at the end the peonies, roses and buddleias, which form the backbone of the border, can be admired all summer. What is interesting from the small-scale gardener's point of view is that this corner faces the drive, where cars sweep in and out every day, all year round, and so it could be easily adapted to a more modest setting. It may form part of a traditional grand-scale border, but the planting is strong and modern and could be used on its own to make an attractive and unusual border which would look particularly good in early spring.

As in other borders in this book where buttresses of evergreen or architectural plants have been used to finish a planting (like the curl of *Hebe subalpina* of Lanning Roper's border in Chapter 22), the bold leaves work well here in rounding off a flowery border. All these techniques are ways of stopping the eye and containing the effect, and this group of perennials with contrasting leaf shapes serves the same purpose.

The crambe forms the high central point to the planting. If the border was an island bed instead of the continuation of a longer feature it would also need something at the centre, which the crambe would provide. However, it does disappear in winter and so *Fatsia japonica* might be a suitable alternative. It has large leaves like the crambe, but it can look rather like the sort of houseplant used in offices and airports and so might not be everyone's choice. A mahonia would be another possibility, or you could change the emphasis of the border by introducing a small tree like the autumn-flowering cherry (*Prunus subhirtella* 'Autumnalis'). Altering one plant in a border can give quite a different character to the whole set-up. It's always rather fun speculating what a garden would look like with a few substitutes and there is no need to assume that anything is sacred if you don't like it, but you do need to choose something with presence if it is to be at the centre of the stage.

Most of the effect here is concentrated in the early months because there is plenty to look at in other parts of the garden as the summer progresses, but the shapes of the leaves remain interesting throughout the year. In late summer the predominant colour, against the green and variegated leaves, is purple from the sage and *Sedum* 'Autumn Joy', as well as from the desir-

OPPOSITE: *The end of a border is seen clearly from the drive, so plants that form bold shapes are chosen for long-range viewing. Euphorbia wulfenii is acid green in spring.*

Paeonia obovata alba has flowers which last only a short time, but the leaves are beautiful enough to be a presence for the rest of the summer.

clumps of finely cut foliage and it would be pretty to see the colchicum appear through these. Late clematis of the *viticella* type could be grown through the bushes of spring-flowering *Spiraea × arguta* and the pinkish-white ribes. As with all plantings there is plenty of fun to be had by adding extra layers of interest, but the bones of this are so good that it would stand perfectly well on its own, which is a great credit to its creator since it is really meant to be seen as part of a larger planting.

LIST OF PLANTS

5 *Aquilegia vulgaris* (columbine: old purple double)
50 *Chionodoxa luciliae*
1 *Chrysanthemum maximum* 'Wirral Pride' (Shasta daisy)
3 *Cosmos atrosanguineus*
1 *Crambe cordifolia*
1 *Euphorbia polychroma*
1 *Euphorbia wulfenii*
3 *Geranium phaeum* 'Album'
3 *Geranium renardii*
3 *Helleborus corsicus*
3 *Holcus mollis* 'Variegata'
5 *Iris pallida* 'Aurea Variegata'
3 *Iris sibirica* (white)
3 *Iris sibirica* 'Caesar' (dark blue)
5 *Lamium orvala* (giant dead nettle; pink)
3 *Lathyrus vernus* (mauve)
3 *Lathyrus vernus* (pink)
5 *Lychnis coronaria* 'Alba'
3 *Nicotiana langsdorffi* (or *N. sylvestris*)
1 *Paeonia obovata alba*
1 *Ribes* 'Albescens' (flowering currant)
1 *Salvia officinalis* 'Purpurascens' (purple sage)
5 *Sedum spectabile* 'Autumn Joy'
1 *Spiraea × arguta*
1 *Thalictrum aquilegifolium*
3 *Veronica gentianoides*

able *Cosmos atrosanguineus*. This relative of the dahlia used to be impossibly scarce and was for a long time on the verge of extinction, but it has now been rescued and, with the discovery that it can be micro-propagated, it should be increasingly easy to find. The cosmos is invaluable in the late summer garden, when velvet-maroon daisy flowers appear for four months on end above good leaves. As an added bonus, the flowers smell of chocolate on warm days and children love them. In southern counties, cosmos has been proved hardy, but as it starts into growth very late in the summer it is often given up for dead. Earlier flowers can be encouraged by taking cuttings and keeping them under glass in winter, so that good sized plants can be set out in May when the danger of frost is past.

The rest of the late summer colour is provided by unusual forms of nicotiana: *N. langsdorffi* produces airy sprays of green bells and *N. sylvestris* is a statuesque white. White annual cosmos (*C. bipinnatus*) might be included for more interest late in the year in gardens which have less to offer than this one, and more bulbs could be planted for spring. There might be room for autumn crocuses (*Colchicum speciosum*) among the columbines. The leaves of these bulbs are fat bright green in spring, but die off depressingly, so they need to be hidden by something else. Cutting down the columbines after flowering produces fresh

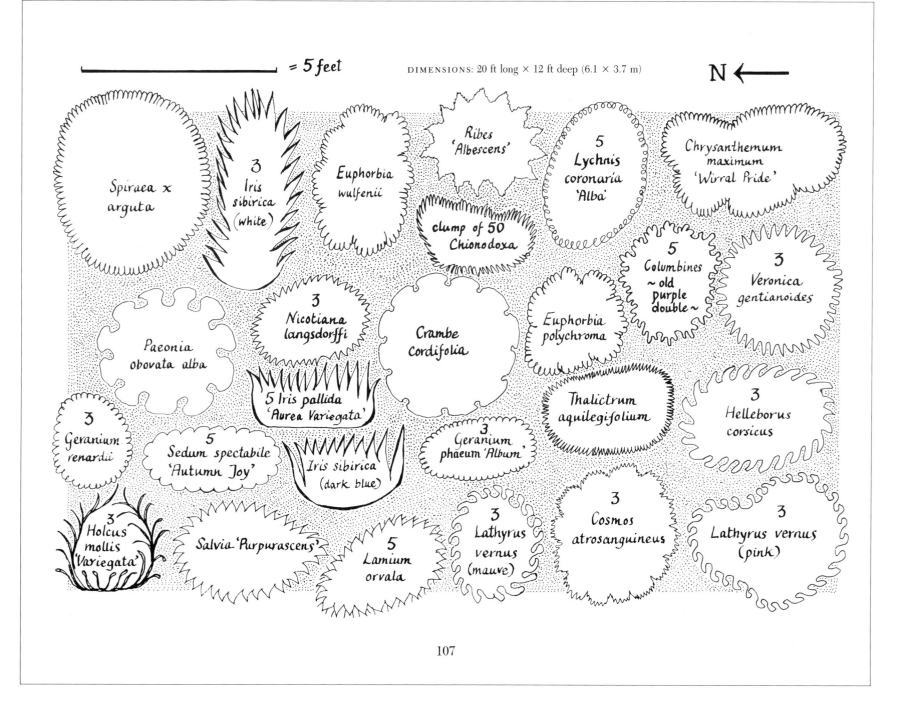

= 5 feet

DIMENSIONS: 20 ft long × 12 ft deep (6.1 × 3.7 m)

N ←

Spiraea x arguta

3 Iris sibirica (white)

Euphorbia wulfenii

Ribes 'Albescens'

5 Lychnis coronaria 'Alba'

Chrysanthemum maximum 'Wirral Pride'

clump of 50 Chionodoxa

5 Columbines ~ old purple double ~

3 Veronica gentianoides

3 Nicotiana langsdorffi

Crambe Cordifolia

Euphorbia polychroma

Paeonia obovata alba

5 Iris pallida 'Aurea Variegata'

Thalictrum aquilegifolium

3 Helleborus corsicus

3 Geranium renardii

5 Sedum spectabile 'Autumn Joy'

Iris sibirica (dark blue)

3 Geranium phaeum 'Album'

3 Holcus mollis 'Variegata'

Salvia 'Purpurascens'

5 Lamium orvala

3 Lathyrus vernus (mauve)

3 Cosmos atrosanguineus

3 Lathyrus vernus (pink)

107

22

EASY AND ELEGANT DOUBLE BORDERS

The late Lanning Roper (1912–83) was a garden designer who helped clients to make plantings which were easy to maintain and pleasant to look at. His work was always pretty but never pretentious and when he helped someone whose taste he respected, the results, as they are here, were particularly good. These Berkshire borders on neutral soil have been maintained in a fairly relaxed way for several years, but show few signs of deterioration and still hold their shape as well as they did originally. Shape was more important to Lanning Roper than colour; he would never have designed, for example, a blue or pink border but planted for firm outlines and contrast of textures. For coherence of design he often recommended repeating good plants along the length of a border, and generally included an evergreen element in any planting. The 'Pfitzerana' junipers were favourites of his and he also liked large-leaved 'punctuation marks' such

as hostas or bergenias, but somehow when Lanning Roper used these clichés of garden design they never seemed commonplace or municipal. Here the *Hebe subalpina* chosen to finish off the borders look rare and distinguished, like the scrolls of banisters on a grand staircase, instead of rather plain as they often do when used by less skilled landscape gardeners. Lanning Roper had a knack of placing quite ordinary plants in ways which made people give them a second look rather than dismissing them as over-used.

The beds of this planting are on a gentle slope and it is interesting to see that the grass path between the borders is wider than the borders themselves. Nine feet is a generous width for a path by any standards, providing the sort of comfortable space where three or four people might stroll before dinner with a drink in hand, for the gardens made by Lanning Roper were essentially for relaxing or being sociable. Although he was a good

plantsman himself, Roper never inflicted gardens which demanded elaborate cultivation on his clients. He gave them simplicity and spaciousness with plantings which never let them down.

Early in the season the borders look good from the house with the bold green sweeps of hebe surrounding pink wands of *Prunus tenella*. There are plenty of crown imperials in shades of bricky red, and marbled pink hellebores under the blossom on the fruit trees. Emerging leaves of peonies uncurl in crimson near the shocking-pink flowers of *Silene* 'Richmond', and this is the time when the pulmonarias and euphorbias are also at their best.

Throughout the summer different sorts of hebes, the lavenders, senecios, rues and silver stachys form a background of strong shape

OPPOSITE: *Gold of lysimachia and the bright pink rose 'Cerise Bouquet' are strong colours, but effective from a distance.*

reducing groups of perennials and introducing flowers like violas or irises to add to the planting the variety which was probably originally intended. However, much of the borders' success is due to their long-established look so it would be a pity to do too much tinkering because they could end up looking bitty and restless. The point of the borders is that they look relaxed and are easy to manage. A little pruning, a little division and an annual mulch of manure for the roses is really all that is required. These are borders to suit non-gardeners, but they are stylish enough to detain and instruct the knowledge-able as well.

Double borders with scrolls of Hebe subalpina *surrounded by lavender lead up to a pair of Scots pines framing a stone urn.*

LIST OF PLANTS

LEFT-HAND BED
7 *Anemone japonica hupehensis* (Japanese anemones)
1 Apple tree 'Charles Ross'
1 *Euphorbia wulfenii*
3 *Hebe albicans*
4 *Hebe subalpina*
5 *Helleborus orientalis* (lenten rose)
2 *Lavandula* 'Hidcote' (lavender)
2 *Lysimachia punctata* (*L. ciliata* for a less invasive substitute)
2 *Nepeta mussinii* 'Six Hills Giant' (catmint)
3 *Origanum vulgare* 'Aureum' (marjoram)
3 *Paeonia officinalis* 'Alba Plena'
1 Pear Tree 'Beurre Hardy'
1 *Prunus tenella* 'Fire Hill' (dwarf almond)
1 *Pulmonaria azurea* 'Munstead Blue'
2 *Rosa* 'Buff Beauty'
1 *Rosa Californica* 'Plena'
1 *Rosa* 'Cerise Bouquet'
1 *Rosa* 'Fantin Latour'

and varying leaf tones to the flowers which come and go. Many of the roses that have been chosen have interesting leaves as well as flowers. *Rosa californica* 'Plena' has a long flowering season and its leaves colour well in autumn; the *rugosa* roses all have good, thick, disease-free leaves and the bushes are covered in hips at the end of the year. 'Cerise Bouquet'

is one of the best modern shrub roses, but is a very strong colour to combine with the brassy yellow lysimachia which is invasive and has probably been increasing in size over the years. Anyone who finds the contrast too great might substitute some hostas (*sieboldiana*) for the clump immediately beneath the 'Cerise Bouquet' rose. There is plenty of scope for

3 *Rosa* 'Iceberg'
1 *Rosa* 'Nevada'
1 *Rosa* 'Souvenir de Philémon Cochet'
6 *Ruta graveolens* 'Jackman's Blue' (rue)
6 *Sedum* 'Autumn Joy'
1 *Senecio greyi*
3 *Silene* 'Richmond' (pink double campion)
3 *Stachys lanata* (lamb's ear)

BETWEEN THE BEDS
6 *Aconitum henryi* (monkshood)
1 Apple tree 'Bramley'
1 *Rosa* 'Frances E. Lester'

RIGHT-HAND BED
1 Apple tree 'Charles Ross'
1 *Buddleia alternifolia*
1 *Geranium endressii* 'Wargrave Pink' (cranesbill)
3 *Geranium* 'Johnson's Blue' (cranesbill)
2 *Hebe albicans*
3 *Hebe subalpina*
3 *Helleborus orientalis*
10 *Iris* 'White City' or 'Cliffs of Dover'
3 *Lavandula* 'Hidcote' (lavender)
2 *Lysimachia punctata* (possible substitute
    L. ciliata)
1 *Nepeta mussinii* 'Six Hills Giant' (catmint)
1 Pear tree 'Beurre Hardy'
1 *Prunus tenella* 'Fire Hill'
1 *Rosa* 'Alba'
1 *Rosa californica* 'Plena'
1 *Rosa* 'Fantin Latour'
3 *Rosa* 'Frau Dagmar Hastrup'
4 *Rosa* 'Iceberg'
1 *Rosa* 'Queen of Denmark'
4 *Ruta* 'Jackman's Blue' (rue)
6 *Sedum* 'Autumn Joy'
2 *Stachys lanata*
3 *Viola cornuta*

Both beds underplanted with:
    Fritillaria imperialis (crown imperials)

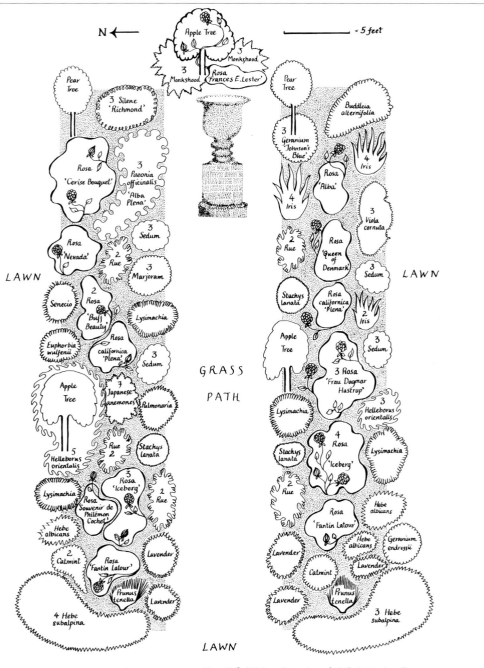

DIMENSIONS OF BOTH BORDERS: 40 × 8 ft (12.2 × 2.4 m), path 9 ft (2.7 m) wide

23

A COLLECTOR'S CORNER

This corner of unusual plants is to be found in the garden attached to one of the best small specialist nurseries in England. On the days when the garden is open for the National Gardens Scheme, would-be purchasers can see how the small specimens in the nursery area will ultimately look and how they can best be combined with other plants. Not everything is out of the ordinary, but forms of even the commonest plants tend to be of the best. As the nursery specializes in snowdrops, winter and early spring are peak periods for effect.

Throughout the winter the conifers provide some colour to look at from the windows of the house. The fronded branches of the cypress are bright brass yellow, while the *Thuja* 'Rheingold' is not at all gold, but bronze in winter and the *T.* 'Boulevard' is an urbane blue. All these small conifers can look less like plants than people, hunched against the cold in expensive coats, but if you are prejudiced against these trees try to think of them as a cheerful joke and then they may not seem so alien. *Acer capillipes* is easier to accommodate. This is the red snake bark maple which can grow as tall as forty feet. The trunk of the tree has a curious, uneven pattern, more netted than striped, but gives a very good effect in winter when it looks as though it has been lightly sprayed with canned frost, and remains this way even on those damp days when everything else is far from sparkling. The two willows can be grown as bushes or as standards. *Salix fargesii* has jolly, red buds in the dark months of the year and its branches are the colour of old mahogany furniture. *Salix × balfourii* is less well known but is worth growing for its outsize catkins and woolly grey leaves. *Salix fargesii* is one of the few willows which resents being pollarded, but the fast-growing *Salix × balfouri* can be kept in scale by annual pruning. Like all willows they prefer damp to dry places. In this planting hybrid roses would be out of place and the rose here, *Rosa pendulina*, is a species which grows in high places throughout Europe. It has single, very early pink flowers, followed by pitcher-shaped fruits rather like the ones which grow on the better known *Rosa moyesii*.

When all these shrubs and trees are fully grown there might not be room for everything, but while they take their time to mature there is still light and space for the variety of perennials underneath. Apart from the dianthus and the erodium, everything is happy in shade, so even as the cover increases from the growing acer there will be no problems about lack of sun. The hellebores flower between the willows in every hue from purple to white. Gardening books always try to claim that these flowers are out for six months of the year;

OPPOSITE: *Willows and conifers seem unlikely companions for spring flowers but provide some interest all winter in a plantsman's garden.*

112

indeed they are paragons, but it is stretching optimism to expect them to last that long. Probably four months is nearer the mark, which is exceptionally long by the standards of most other flowers, especially when the months include January and February. There are plenty of bulbs out after the New Year: snowdrops and small narcissi, including the very early *N.* 'Cedric Morris' and *N. minor*, jonquils and scillas. Large bulbs like daffodils are always out of place in flowerbeds because of the problem of their unsightly dying leaves. Here the solution is to plant hostas, whose leaves spread decently over the remains of the bulbs, shading them from the sun and gradually filling all the space occupied by the earlier flowers.

Thermopsis is not very well known but it is pretty and not difficult, with clear, yellow pea-flowers in early summer. The bushy spring-flowering lathyrus is another member of the pea family which forms dense little mounds of green covered in pink flowers. The double columbines are dark terracotta with green-tipped petals, and the fritillaries suit the same sombre colour scheme. The white-flowered, variegated form of honesty seeds itself in the bed and later a stand of tiger lilies dominates the planting. It's all rather distinguished and unusual: a collector's corner with plenty of things that require close inspection and a few to look at from far away.

LEFT: *The variegated form of the white honesty lights up dark shrubs. Once introduced it becomes self-perpetuating.*

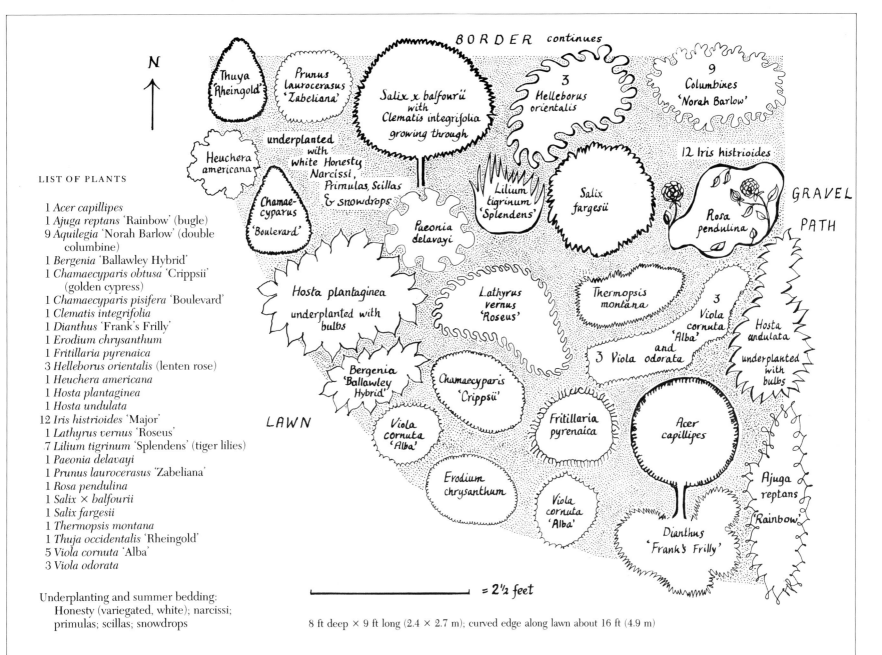

N

LIST OF PLANTS

1 *Acer capillipes*
1 *Ajuga reptans* 'Rainbow' (bugle)
9 *Aquilegia* 'Norah Barlow' (double
    columbine)
1 *Bergenia* 'Ballawley Hybrid'
1 *Chamaecyparis obtusa* 'Crippsii'
    (golden cypress)
1 *Chamaecyparis pisifera* 'Boulevard'
1 *Clematis integrifolia*
1 *Dianthus* 'Frank's Frilly'
1 *Erodium chrysanthum*
1 *Fritillaria pyrenaica*
3 *Helleborus orientalis* (lenten rose)
1 *Heuchera americana*
1 *Hosta plantaginea*
1 *Hosta undulata*
12 *Iris histrioides* 'Major'
1 *Lathyrus vernus* 'Roseus'
7 *Lilium tigrinum* 'Splendens' (tiger lilies)
1 *Paeonia delavayi*
1 *Prunus laurocerasus* 'Zabeliana'
1 *Rosa pendulina*
1 *Salix × balfourii*
1 *Salix fargesii*
1 *Thermopsis montana*
1 *Thuja occidentalis* 'Rheingold'
5 *Viola cornuta* 'Alba'
3 *Viola odorata*

Underplanting and summer bedding:
    Honesty (variegated, white); narcissi;
    primulas; scillas; snowdrops

Diagram labels:

B O R D E R continues

Thuya 'Rheingold'
Prunus laurocerasus 'Zabeliana'
Salix x balfourii with Clematis integrifolia growing through
3 Helleborus orientalis
9 Columbines 'Norah Barlow'
Heuchera americana
underplanted with white Honesty Narcissi, Primulas, Scillas & snowdrops
Chamae-cyparus 'Boulevard'
12 Iris histrioides
Lilium tigrinum 'Splendens'
Salix fargesii
Rosa pendulina
GRAVEL PATH
Paeonia delavayi
Hosta plantaginea underplanted with bulbs
Lathyrus vernus 'Roseus'
Thermopsis montana
3 Viola cornuta 'Alba' and 3 Viola odorata
Hosta undulata underplanted with bulbs
Bergenia 'Ballawley Hybrid'
Chamaecyparis 'Crippsii'
Viola cornuta 'Alba'
Fritillaria pyrenaica
Acer capillipes
LAWN
Erodium chrysanthum
Viola cornuta 'Alba'
Dianthus 'Frank's Frilly'
Ajuga reptans 'Rainbow'

= 2½ feet

8 ft deep × 9 ft long (2.4 × 2.7 m); curved edge along lawn about 16 ft (4.9 m)

115

24

IMPRESSIONIST COLOUR IN A COUNTRY-HOUSE BORDER

This double border in a steeply sloping, cold garden, over limestone on the side of a Yorkshire dale, was laid out between the wars and has hardly been altered since. The effect in late summer and early autumn is of simple, unimproved flowers in yellows, pinks and oranges toned down by patches of misty blue. The whole thing looks like an impressionist painting, with huge patches of colour blurring into each other in the tradition of one of Gertrude Jekyll's borders. The area is, in fact, twice the length of the plan shown but it would be possible to achieve a similar effect by planting on the scale illustrated. It is not, however, something to attempt in a small space. It is interesting to note that the preferred dimensions of Miss Jekyll's borders were 200 by 18 feet, so although this double border looks grand by modern standards, measuring 130 feet in length and 9 feet wide, it is roughly only half the size of one of hers.

Groups of delphiniums planted along the back of the border start to flower after the cottage peonies are over, while the rest of the plants are still only clumps of green. This is perhaps the only way to grow delphiniums – behind perennials which will hide their awkward dying and cover the gap that they leave. Here, it does not matter if they are left after the flowers fade, but in a more conspicuous position they could be cut to the ground after flowering and induced to bloom a second time using plenty of water and liquid feed. Gertrude Jekyll recommended cutting off the flower heads and reducing the clumps to a height of four feet, so that they could then act as a host for a late-flowering climber which had been trained through the stems from behind. She suggested *Clematis flammula*, which is white and scented, flowering in September, but in this sort of colour scheme nasturtiums are not to be despised.

Most of the plants chosen have proved their worth by lasting for so many years. They may not be the latest novelty from the plant breeders, but for their old-fashioned reliability they deserve to be treated with respect. However there are one or two things which might be better discarded: *Aster acris* is a Michaelmas daisy with small flowers and a habit of looking lanky, so for this reason several clumps of it have been replaced on the plan by *Aster × frikartii* 'Mönch', which has one of the longest flowering seasons of any perennial. The other alteration to the border might be the addition of a fourth musk rose, 'Cornelia', at the edge of the bed behind the lavender. There always were musks in the border and most of the ones that remain were originally introduced into the garden from the collection of the Reverend Joseph Pemberton, who raised many of these useful long-flowering hybrids. It seems appropriate to restore

OPPOSITE: *Drifts of orange and purple daisies blazing into autumn in an old-fashioned double herbaceous border.*

'Cornelia' to her position for the sake of symmetry. The borders are not matched, but it gives them a framework to repeat the plants at either end and to see clumps of the larger ones at regular intervals along each bed. What is remarkable is that the effect has remained more or less the same for fifty summers, the balance of the border has been maintained by regular division and, over the years, only the odd change has been made. The rambler roses on the trellis at the back have suffered a little and could be replaced by stronger varieties which have a longer flowering season, but even this might be a mistake. Modern plantings rarely evoke the understated and settled charm of a border like this, a traditional high-summer collection of flowers which has stood the test of time and resisted passing fashion.

LEFT: *The white form of* Anemone japonica *flowers for almost three months and can become invasive after a slow start in life.*

LIST OF PLANTS

BED A
3 *Aconitum henryi* (monkshood)
25 *Anemone japonica* 'Honorine Jobert'
3 *Aster acris* (old Michaelmas daisy)
7 *Aster × frikartii* 'Mönch'
3 *Aster* 'Little Pink Lady'
1 *Berberis thunbergii* 'Atropurpurea'
9 *Crocosmia* 'Citronella'
17 *Delphinium* Pacific Hybrids (blue)
10 *Galega officinalis*
7 *Geranium* 'Johnson's Blue' (cranesbill)
5 *Helenium autumnale* 'The Bishop'
3 *Helenium autumnale* 'Moerheim Beauty'
7 *Helenium rubrum* (bronze)
5 *Helianthus* 'Miss Mellish'
10 *Lavandula vera* (Dutch lavender)
4 *Lythrum salicaria* (purple loosestrife 'Brightness')

9 *Paeonia officinalis* 'Rubra Plena'
3 *Phlox paniculata* 'Fujiyama'
3 *Phlox paniculata* 'Mother of Pearl'
2 *Rosa* 'Cornelia'
1 *Rosa* 'Sammy' (hybrid musk)
1 *Rosa* 'Thisbe'
1 *Spiraea* 'Anthony Waterer'

BED B
3 *Anaphalis triplinervis*
7 *Anemone japonica* 'Honorine Jobert'
5 *Aster acris*
7 *Aster × frikartii* 'Mönch'
1 *Berberis thunbergii* 'Atropurpurea'
3 *Chrysanthemum uliginosum*
9 *Crocosmia masonorum* (possible substitute 'Citronella')
12 *Delphinium* Pacific Hybrids (blue)
5 *Galega officinalis*

5 *Helenium autumnale* 'The Bishop'
5 *Helenium autumnale* 'Bruno' (late bronze)
3 *Helenium autumnale* 'Moerheim Beauty'
6 *Helenium rubrum*
3 *Helianthus* 'Miss Mellish'
6 *Lavandula vera*
7 *Linum narbonense* (flax)
5 *Lysimachia ciliata*
3 *Lythrum salicaria*
5 *Monarda didyma* 'Croftway Pink' (bergamot)
5 *Nepeta mussinii* (catmint)
5 *Oenothera biennis* (evening primrose)
3 *Phlox paniculata* 'Fujiyama'
3 *Phlox paniculata* 'Mother of Pearl'
2 *Rosa* 'Cornelia'
1 *Rosa* 'Nuits de Young' (moss)
2 *Rosa* 'Thisbe'
1 *Rosa* 'Wilhelm'
3 *Sidalcea* 'Sussex Beauty'

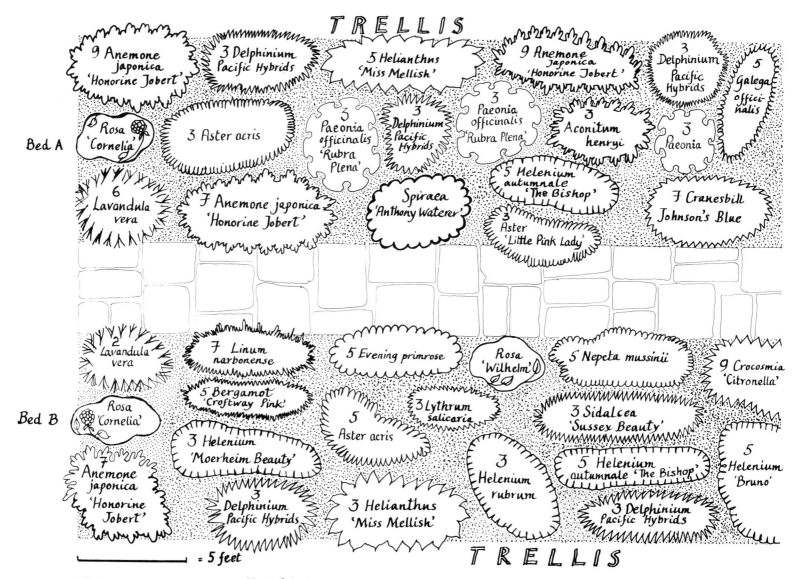

TRELLIS

Bed A

9 Anemone japonica 'Honorine Jobert'

3 Delphinium Pacific Hybrids

5 Helianthus 'Miss Mellish'

9 Anemone japonica 'Honorine Jobert'

3 Delphinium Pacific Hybrids

5 Galega officinalis

Rosa 'Cornelia'

3 Aster acris

3 Paeonia officinalis 'Rubra Plena'

3 Delphinium Pacific Hybrids

3 Paeonia officinalis 'Rubra Plena'

3 Aconitum henryi

3 Paeonia

6 Lavandula vera

7 Anemone japonica 'Honorine Jobert'

Spiraea 'Anthony Waterer'

5 Helenium autumnale 'The Bishop'

7 Cranesbill Johnson's Blue

3 Aster 'Little Pink Lady'

Bed B

2 Lavandula vera

7 Linum narbonense

5 Evening primrose

Rosa 'Wilhelm'

5 Nepeta mussinii

9 Crocosmia 'Citronella'

5 Bergamot 'Croftway Pink'

5 Aster acris

3 Lythrum salicaria

3 Sidalcea 'Sussex Beauty'

Rosa 'Cornelia'

3 Helenium 'Moerheim Beauty'

3 Helenium rubrum

5 Helenium autumnale 'The Bishop'

5 Helenium 'Bruno'

7 Anemone japonica 'Honorine Jobert'

3 Delphinium Pacific Hybrids

3 Helianthus 'Miss Mellish'

3 Delphinium Pacific Hybrids

TRELLIS

⊢———⊣ = 5 feet

DIMENSIONS OF BOTH BORDERS: 65 × 9 ft (19.8 × 2.7 m), divided by a 4 ft (1.2 m) wide flagstone path

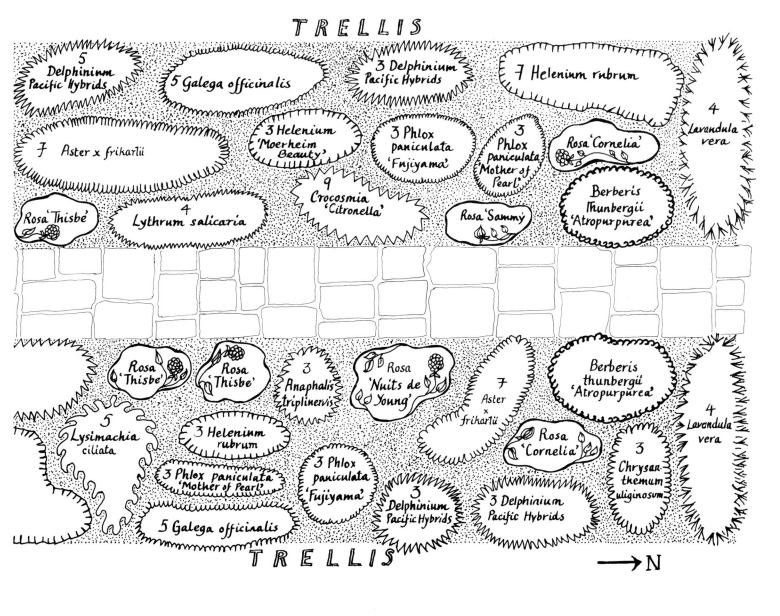

TRELLIS

5 Delphinium Pacific Hybrids

5 Galega officinalis

3 Delphinium Pacific Hybrids

7 Helenium rubrum

4 Lavandula vera

7 Aster x frikartii

3 Helenium 'Moerheim Beauty'

3 Phlox paniculata 'Fujiyama'

3 Phlox paniculata 'Mother of Pearl'

Rosa 'Cornelia'

9 Crocosmia 'Citronella'

Rosa 'Thisbe'

4 Lythrum salicaria

Rosa 'Sammy'

Berberis Thunbergii 'Atropurpurea'

Rosa 'Thisbe'

Rosa 'Thisbe'

3 Anaphalis triplinervis

Rosa 'Nuits de Young'

7 Aster x frikartii

Berberis thunbergii 'Atropurpurea'

5 Lysimachia ciliata

3 Helenium rubrum

Rosa 'Cornelia'

4 Lavandula vera

3 Phlox paniculata 'Mother of Pearl'

3 Phlox paniculata 'Fujiyama'

3 Delphinium Pacific Hybrids

3 Delphinium Pacific Hybrids

3 Chrysanthemum uliginosum

5 Galega officinalis

TRELLIS

→ N

25

THE 'MINGLED' BORDER

The Gardens Adviser to The National Trust is responsible for seeing that there is something to look at from Easter until October in all of the Trust's gardens. At home he aims for the same results, but practises an uncommon method of planting in one of the borders to maintain his private display. The 'mingled' border relies on a very few structural plants with a liberal scattering of perennials and bulbs which are reproduced down the length of the border and which succeed each other throughout the year. This successional gardening is occasionally practised on a larger scale, where repeated clumps of shrubs or plants produce a dominant theme, which is then replaced by another set piece. The famous border at New College, Oxford, has clumps of *Prunus tenella* and a good, dark-red ribes arranged down the bed in early spring. Later in the year the focus changes to patches of giant catmint or salvias and finally to buddleias and dahlias. This is one way of produc-

ing a consistent theme which changes with the seasons, but it needs a lot of space.

In herbaceous borders you sometimes see a more economical way of achieving the same effect where two perennials are interplanted, so that as the first lot of flowers and stems die down, the second tier rises through the fading plants to produce different flowers in the same place. Oriental poppies followed by aconitums, or irises succeeded by the airy blue flax are two examples of companions which can co-exist. The principles of both these types of planting are the same in this border: there is a dominant theme from shrubs; ceanothus and tree wisteria first, followed by 'Iceberg' roses and then by the bushes of species fuchsia, and between these and other smaller shrubs there is a complicated layering of perennials and bulbs, so that the border always appears evenly coloured in misty shades of blue with occasional touches of white.

The bed is backed by a beech hedge and parted by a wide grass path, on either side of which are round-headed trees (*Acer platanoides* 'Globosum'). Stopping the end of the longer section is a terracotta urn flanked by two standard wisterias and surrounded by rue. The middle of the bed would appear rather featureless, apart from a few clumps of irises, if it were not for the fact that there is always something in flower. Most gardeners lean heavily on structural plants to tide them over the non-flowering patches, but if you can provide a continuously changing pattern of colour this becomes less important. Relentless rows of bedding plants would not produce the same effect at all. This is a subtle arrangement of shifting tones and shades which could never bore the onlooker.

OPPOSITE: *The misty effect of this mingled border lasts all summer, as flowers succeed one another in waves of blue.*

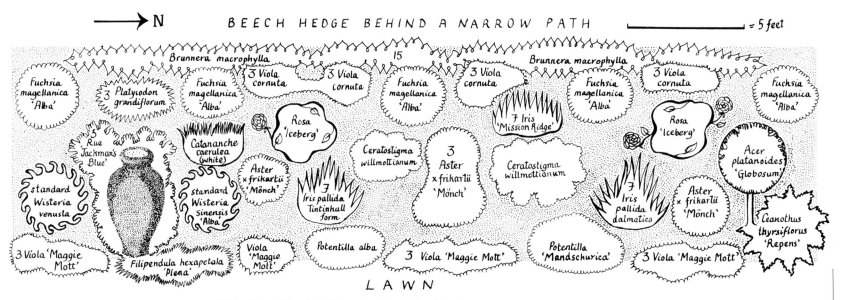

DIMENSIONS: left-hand bed 35 × 8 ft (10.7 × 2.4 m); right-hand bed 10 × 8 ft (3 × 2.4 m); path 8 ft (2.4 m) wide

Planting is tricky. It would be best to put in the plants marked on the plan, followed by the bulbs which are distributed all over the bed and then to space out the rest of the perennials as evenly as possible, keeping the anemones and *Campanula latiloba* towards the back. The liatris is also tall, but slender, so the occasional stray at the front would not matter too much. *Geranium* 'Buxton's Blue' takes up very little room until late summer and can be planted to ramble over clumps of low-spreading plants which have flowered earlier in the year, such as the arabis, myosotis or hyssop. Everything else needs to be fitted in according to taste and space.

LIST OF PLANTS

SPRING
20 *Brunnera macrophylla*
 2 *Ceanothus thyrsiflorus* 'Repens'
 1 *Potentilla alba* (in clumps)
12 *Viola cornuta*
10 *Viola* 'Maggie Mott'
 1 *Wisteria sinensis* 'Alba'
 1 *Wisteria venusta*

Underplanting and summer bedding:
 5 *Arabis albida* 'Flore Pleno'
100 *Chionodoxa luciliae*
 50 *Leucojum aestivum*
100 *Muscari armeniacum*
100 *Muscari armeniacum* 'Album'
100 *Muscari* 'Blue Spike'
200 *Myosotis alpestris*

LATE SPRING/EARLY SUMMER
 1 *Filipendula hexapetula* 'Plena' (meadowsweet)
14 *Iris* 'Mission Ridge'
 7 *Iris pallida dalmatica*
 7 *Iris pallida* (Tintinhull form)
 (*Potentilla alba* and *Viola* 'Maggie Mott' still out)

Underplanted with:
 4 *Campanula latiloba* 'Alba'
 4 *Campanula latiloba* 'Hidcote Amethyst'
 4 *Campanula latiloba* 'High Cliffe'
 1 *Lychnis flos-cuculi* (white ragged robin)

SUMMER
 3 *Platycodon grandiflorum*
 1 *Potentilla* 'Mandschurica'
 3 *Rosa* 'Iceberg'

124

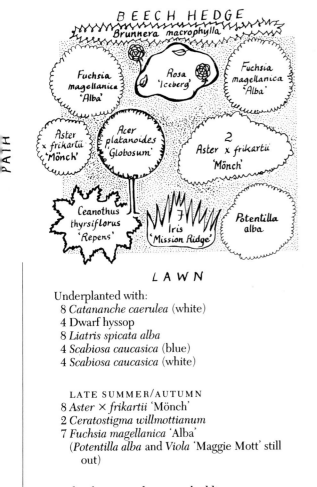

BEECH HEDGE

Brunnera macrophylla

Fuchsia magellanica 'Alba'

Rosa 'Iceberg'

Fuchsia magellanica 'Alba'

Aster × frikartii 'Mönch'

Acer platanoides 'Globosum'

2 *Aster × frikartii 'Mönch'*

Ceanothus thyrsiflorus 'Repens'

Iris 'Mission Ridge'

Potentilla alba

LAWN

Underplanted with:
8 *Catananche caerulea* (white)
4 Dwarf hyssop
8 *Liatris spicata alba*
4 *Scabiosa caucasica* (blue)
4 *Scabiosa caucasica* (white)

LATE SUMMER/AUTUMN
8 *Aster × frikartii* 'Mönch'
2 *Ceratostigma willmottianum*
7 *Fuchsia magellanica* 'Alba'
   (*Potentilla alba* and *Viola* 'Maggie Mott' still
   out)

Underplanting and summer bedding:
15 *Anemone japonica* 'Honorine Jobert'
 1 *Geranium wallichianum* 'Buxton's Blue'

Foliage:
 2 *Acer platanoides* 'Globosum'
 5 *Ruta* 'Jackman's Blue'

Campanulas are out at the same time as the creamy white meadowsweet,
seen against a terracotta 'Ali Baba' jar.

125

26

WINTER PLANTING AROUND A TREE

People rarely think of putting flowerbeds round trees. Waves of golden daffodils lapping the trunks of cherry or apple trees are common enough, but it is unusual to find a tree surrounded by anything but grass for the major part of the year. Competing with their roots is hard work for plants – apart from some bulbs which can make their own arrangements for storing energy – but this arrangement of a raised bed is a neat way to solve the problem and give the smaller plants their fair share. The open branches of fruit trees make them suitable for this kind of treatment; those which cast a really dense shade, such as chestnut or cherry, might make it too dark for anything else to grow. As this is in a woodland garden, it is easy to find logs for retaining the bed; in other places natural stone or weathered brick (built to a height of about two feet) could take the place of wood. Nothing too formal and nothing that jars with the setting should be the aim. Once the bed is raised and filled with a good mixture of compost and earth, plants feel quite differently about appearing in company with trees.

The centrepiece here is an old apple tree, whose point is not that it bears apples but that it acts as host for that cliché of country-house gardening, the tree-climbing rose. In this case not the inevitable 'Kiftsgate', but 'Frances E. Lester', the rambler which, as garden-writer Graham Stuart Thomas declares, 'fills the garden with the intense fragrance of oranges and bananas'. Although the smell of bananas, luckily, has escaped this nose, the roses do look like the best sort of appleblossom. A honeysuckle (*Lonicera ciliosa*) shares the tree with *Rosa* 'Mrs Lester'. This is an American climber with an early flowering in June. An alternative might be *Lonicera tragophylla* which flowers for longer and is much more showy, but perhaps this oriental might be overwhelming in a quiet woodland setting.

Most of the plants are subdued and all of them like the shade. A little sunlight reaches one side of the circle, but not much. The different greens of ornamental laurels and hellebores, as well as the ivies and other evergreen shrubs, tide the planting over the months between the time when the lilies and cyclamen are over and the aconites begin. In summer the feathery leaves of the robinia appear above the darker, heavier evergreens and its pink flowers show up against this background. The robinia is a rather brittle-looking shrub and really likes a sunnier place than this, but in some situations a sparse crop of flowers can look better than too many and this is probably the case here. The garden belongs to a plantsman who prefers species and single flowers to doubles and hybrids, so it is important that this bed fits in with everything else.

OPPOSITE: *A raised bed round a tree can support a variety of plants.*

Lenten roses come in all shades of pink, purple and white and are in flower for three cold winter months.

The bulbs chosen are the smallest forms of narcissi, all sorts of cyclamen, two forms of aconite which flower in succession and plenty of snowdrops and scillas. From January until April, bulbs appear and disappear in thick patches of colour which are covered later by ferns and hostas. The hellebores flower during the same dreary period as the bulbs, so there is plenty to admire in the nastiest months of the year.

In summer the lilies revel in the good drainage which the raised bed provides. *Szovitsianum* is a tall turkscap lily with pale yellow flowers which will tolerate chalk and thrives in this bed of limey soil lavishly mixed with rotted horse manure. Almost everything seeds itself in these conditions and weeds are easy to control. Not everyone has access to unlimited manure, but plenty of peat mixed with a balanced fertilizer ought to produce similar conditions.

The thing that usually defeats people who try planting under trees is the dryness. Plenty of plants like light shade, but there are far fewer which can put up with a combination of shade and drought. Making a raised bed means a much wider choice of things to grow and gives the tree a new lease of life; it also provides extra space in gardens which seem to have run out of room. Plants for winter, like plain children in a team game, are always the last to be chosen; letting them have a place of their own under a tree spoils no summer flower's display and gives the winter ones a chance to show what they can really do.

LIST OF PLANTS

3 *Asplenium scolopendrium* (hart's-tongue fern)
3 *Blechnum penna-marina* (fern)
1 *Campanula pocharskyana*
1 *Dryopteris polystichum aculcatum* (hard shield
   fern)
6 *Helleborus foetidus* (stinking hellebore)
20 *Helleborus orientalis* (lenten rose)
1 *Lonicera ciliosa* (honeysuckle)
1 *Mahonia aquifolium* 'Undulata'
3 *Polypodium* 'Cambricum' (fern)
1 *Prunus laurocerasus* 'Otto Luyken'
1 *Prunus laurocerasus* 'Zabeliana'
1 *Robinia kelseyi*
1 *Rosa* 'Frances E. Lester'
1 *Ruscus aculeatus* (butcher's broom)
1 *Skimmia japonica* 'Fragrans'

Underplanting and summer bedding:
50 *Chionodoxa luciliae*
50 *Crocus tomasinianus*
10 *Cyclamen coum*
10 *Cyclamen hederifolium*
50 *Eranthis* × 'Guinea Gold' (aconite)
50 *Eranthis hyemalis* (aconite)
50 *Galanthus* (snowdrop) in variety, including
    elwesii and *caucasicus*
 9 *Hosta* in variety (*elata, fortunei, sieboldiana,
    ventricosa*)
12 *Lilium szovitsianum*
50 *Narcissus cyclamineus* and *N. triandrus* (hybrids)
50 *Scilla bifolia* and *S. tubergeniana*

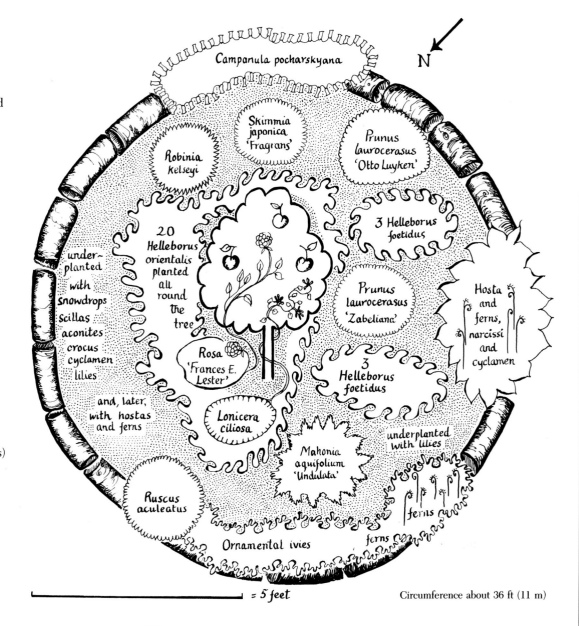

27

Golden Shrubs for a Dark Setting

Dry ground dominated by a large cedar tree is not the ideal place to garden and in this narrow border under a stone wall it is a surprise to see such a fresh and spring-like effect. Pale gold bushes of *Philadelphus* 'Aureus' dominate the planting early in the year. Unfortunately they do not hold their colour for the rest of the season, but turn green as the year advances. In gloomy places under similar conditions where the golden leaves seem desirable for longer periods, golden privet would be worth considering but, although the effect would last, it would look brassier than the philadelphus. More golden elder might be another possibility, but it would perhaps be a pity to lose the matchless scent of the philadelphus flowers, which neither privet nor elder would provide. Later in the year the variegated leaves of irises, brunnera and hostas keep the pale theme going, so that against the dark background there is always an impression of light.

In spring the euphorbias, doronicums and cheiranthus all produce cheerful yellow flowers, making the whole bed look sunny, while various primroses and cowslips add more patches of gold. The old *Primula* 'Gold Lace' grows here, as well as double primroses, none of which are easy to manage in such dry conditions; they all need dividing after flowering and ideally would prefer to spend the summer in a darker, richer position to build up their strength for the following year. However, clay soils do hold some of the moisture they like and they will survive with a mulch in a cool, dry spot. Flashes of yellow are not so frequent after the spring is over but the rose 'Golden Showers' produces flowers which suggest sunshine, and more light is reflected off the white blooms of *Hydrangea* 'Grandiflora'. Like the primulas, this shrub and the violas at the front of the border normally prefer damper positions but with a little encouragement can be induced to flower well.

Polemoniums are pretty but neglected flowers which always do well in the shade. The white form found here has a long flowering season and airy-looking leaves of a fresh green. To produce more flowers in larger borders, white foxgloves, white tobacco plants and cranesbills might all be introduced.

Problem places are often planted with a strong ground-cover element where things like bergenias and ferns prevail, which can look rather heavy and dull; what is interesting about this border is that it manages to seem flowery and light for most of the year.

The plan shows only half the length of the planting under the wall which is broken by a flight of steps. The half not shown is very similar in feeling to the one described. At each end and slightly in front of these beds are two silver-leafed pear trees surrounded

OPPOSITE: *The golden form of the ordinary philadelphus shows up in the shade of cedars in spring, but reverts to green later in the year.*

by small squares of box, which in summer are filled with white petunias. The architectural definition which these give to the narrow beds under the wall is a great help and it is often worth remembering that where there is not much room for a bold effect, sometimes a strong outline, like a box hedge along the edge of a border, or a note of formality, like the square beds used here, will often help to pull the design together.

A difficult bed in dry shade need not be dull, or let down the rest of the garden.

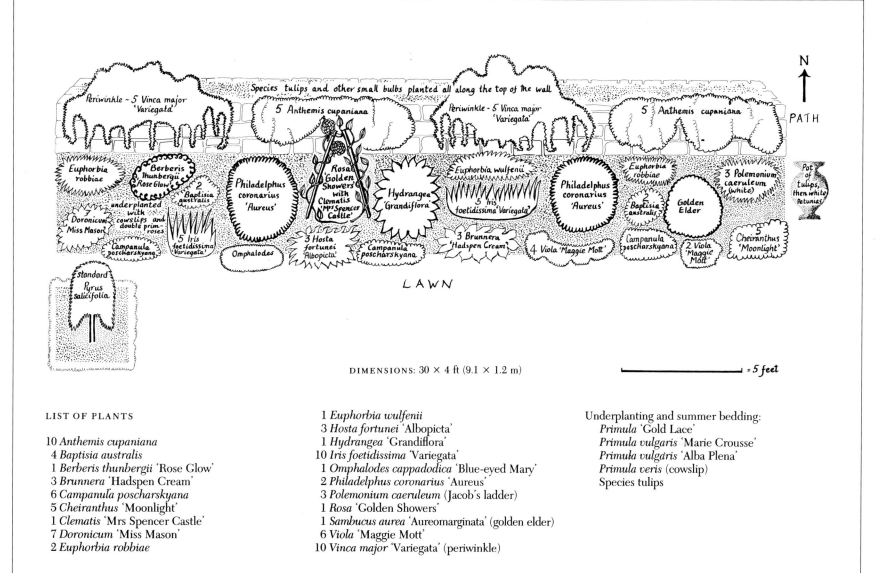

Periwinkle ~ 5 Vinca major 'Variegata'

Species tulips and other small bulbs planted all along the top of the wall

5 Anthemis cupaniana

Periwinkle ~ 5 Vinca major 'Variegata'

5 Anthemis cupaniana

N

PATH

Euphorbia robbiae

Berberis thunbergii 'Rose Glow'

2 Baptisia australis

underplanted with cowslips and double primroses

7 Doronicum 'Miss Mason'

Campanula poscharskyana

Standard Pyrus Salicifolia

Philadelphus coronarius 'Aureus'

5 Iris foetidissima 'Variegata'

Omphalodes

Rosa 'Golden Showers' with Clematis 'Mrs Spencer Castle'

3 Hosta fortunei 'Albopicta'

Campanula poscharskyana

Hydrangea 'Grandiflora'

Euphorbia wulfenii

5 Iris foetidissima 'Variegata'

3 Brunnera 'Hadspen Cream'

Philadelphus coronarius 'Aureus'

2 Baptisia australis

Golden Elder

4 Viola 'Maggie Mott'

Euphorbia robbiae

Campanula poscharskyana

2 Viola 'Maggie Mott'

3 Polemonium caeruleum (white)

Cheiranthus 'Moonlight'

Pot of tulips, then white Petunias

LAWN

DIMENSIONS: 30 × 4 ft (9.1 × 1.2 m)

= 5 feet

LIST OF PLANTS

10 *Anthemis cupaniana*
 4 *Baptisia australis*
 1 *Berberis thunbergii* 'Rose Glow'
 3 *Brunnera* 'Hadspen Cream'
 6 *Campanula poscharskyana*
 5 *Cheiranthus* 'Moonlight'
 1 *Clematis* 'Mrs Spencer Castle'
 7 *Doronicum* 'Miss Mason'
 2 *Euphorbia robbiae*

 1 *Euphorbia wulfenii*
 3 *Hosta fortunei* 'Albopicta'
 1 *Hydrangea* 'Grandiflora'
10 *Iris foetidissima* 'Variegata'
 1 *Omphalodes cappadodica* 'Blue-eyed Mary'
 2 *Philadelphus coronarius* 'Aureus'
 3 *Polemonium caeruleum* (Jacob's ladder)
 1 *Rosa* 'Golden Showers'
 1 *Sambucus aurea* 'Aureomarginata' (golden elder)
 6 *Viola* 'Maggie Mott'
10 *Vinca major* 'Variegata' (periwinkle)

Underplanting and summer bedding:
  Primula 'Gold Lace'
  Primula vulgaris 'Marie Crousse'
  Primula vulgaris 'Alba Plena'
  Primula veris (cowslip)
  Species tulips

133

28

A STRONG COLOUR BORDER

Graham Stuart Thomas is an artist and a plantsman. He was probably the first person to recognize the changing needs of twentieth-century gardeners, for he pioneered the use of ground-cover plants to help people who were suddenly faced with doing all their own outside work. In his gardens he stresses the importance of foliage and concentrates on growing those things which are best suited to the soil and setting. In his books he continues to recommend thoughtful planting and the exercise of taste. His experience of making gardens – particularly for the National Trust, whose Gardens Consultant he remains – is formidable, as is his knowledge of plants. Graham Thomas's own garden is a complicated cornucopia of rare plants, but this border designed for Lytes Cary does not contain too many unobtainables and is fairly straightforward to plant.

The original border was designed by Graham Thomas. The other plan illustrates the changes that have been made over the years by the present tenant of Lytes Cary, Jeremy Chittenden, with the help of James Marshall who is Assistant Gardens Adviser at the Trust and landscape architect Paul Miles. This is the only border in the book which is documented at two stages of its existence and the comparison shows what an ephemeral business gardening always is. Even an institution like The National Trust, with all the skills needed to maintain a good planting, is forced to make changes. For example, at Lytes Cary plants such as the *Aster × frikartii* have completely disappeared. Clumps of these long-flowering blue Michaelmas daisies have made way for a low-growing ceanothus, a clump of yellow montbretia and a group of striped 'Rosa Mundi' roses. A dwarf berberis has gone from the front and has been replaced by irises. Aconitum and delphiniums have been added, as well as some hibiscus and more fuchsias for late-summer effect. The soil is heavy, cold clay and roses obviously do well so there are more of them now than there were originally, while the salvias, which like well-drained soil, seem to have faded out.

There has been an interesting shift of colour. In the original plan the large group of purple berberis was surrounded by magenta and red roses, with the lovely crimson scabious (*rumelica*) in front. This is much more like the colour schemes favoured by Russell Page than the later version, where yellow roses have crept in to replace the magenta ones and the latter have been moved up next to the red to make a strong group with the purple rhus. In both borders there are yellow roses against a purple background of rhus. The size of the shrub keeps the yellow and red roses apart, so it does not look as brash as it sounds, but this contrast of yellow with purple obviously has a hold on some designers.

OPPOSITE: *Clumps of well-grown plants cover the ground in rich Persian-rug colours.*

Sedum *'Autumn Joy'* is a good plant for
butterflies and its flowers hold their colour well
into the summer.

136

The colours in both borders are strong, but in the earlier version they look as though they might have been better orchestrated. There is a much busier feeling about the recent additions and changes, which makes for a livelier looking border, but the earlier one was probably more restful. The width of the bed is not large and a feature of Graham Thomas's work in narrow borders is that shrubs are never graded to the back of a border but run forward like headlands into the sea, so that the whole bed cannot be seen at once. Large shrubs make bays for smaller plants; they keep the colours in separate compartments and also provide shelter for tender things. Another trick which Graham Thomas uses is to introduce a collection of one plant (in this case some sedums) and then add a stray plant a little further away, so that it looks as though it had seeded itself from the main clump.

The present border is at its best in early July although, as in all gardens which are open to the public, it has to look good from April to October. All the fuchsias in it are hardy and, with the exception of the Rose 'Holstein' which is now unobtainable, few of the plants should be hard to find. The white *Agapanthus* 'Alice Gloucester' might prove evasive, in which case more day lilies can be substituted. Not everyone has the chance to have an original Graham Stuart Thomas border in their garden and it would be tempting to plant the first version on rich but well-drained soil, in front of a grey stone wall, to see what it looked like in ten years from now.

LIST OF PLANTS

(5) 8 *Achillea* 'Moonshine'°
6 *Agapanthus campanulatus*
8 *Anemone hupehensis japonica* 'September Charm' (common pink)
(13) 22 *Aster × frikartii*
(4) 13 *Berberis thunbergii* 'Atropurpurea Nana'
1 *Clematis* 'Gipsy Queen'
1 *Clematis* 'Jackmanii Alba'
2 *Clematis* 'Perle d'Azur'
1 *Clematis* 'Royal Velours'
1 *Clematis tangutica*
1 *Clematis viticella* 'Abundance'
1 *Cornus alba* 'Spaethii Aurea'
1 *Cydonia japonica* (flowering quince)
6 *Echinops ritro*
6 *Eryngium tripartitum*
(6) 12 *Fuchsia gracilis tricolor*
(4) 6 *Fuchsia* 'Mrs Popple'
5 *Hemerocallis* 'Pink Damask' (day lily)
5 *Iris* 'Cambridge Blue'
(5) 8 *Lavandula* 'Hidcote Giant'
(3) 6 *Lavandula vera* (Dutch lavender)
7 *Nepeta gigantea* (catmint)
5 *Nepeta mussinii* (catmint)
(8) 12 *Penstemon* 'Garnet'
3 *Polygonum amplexicaule* 'Atrosanguineum'
4 *Potentilla arbuscula*
4 *Potentilla* 'Gibson's Scarlet'
6 *Potentilla* 'Primrose Dame' (primrose beauty)
(1) 3 *Rhus cotinus* 'Foliis purpureis' 'Notcutt's Variety' (now called *Cotinus coggyria*)
5 *Rosa* 'Allgold'
(1) 2 *Rosa rubrifolia*
1 *Rosa* 'Allen Chandler'
2 *Rosa* 'Buff Beauty'
4 *Rosa* 'Elmshorn'

7 *Rosa* 'Yellow Holstein' ('Allgold' substitute)
5 *Rosa* 'Magenta'
(4) 6 *Rosa* 'Rosemary Rose'
(5) 7 *Salvia* 'East Friesland' (or *S. × superba*)
(7) 15 *Salvia officinalis* 'Purpurascens' (purple sage)
(12) 17 *Salvia × superba*
4 *Scabiosa rumelica* (syn. *Knautia macedonica*)
5 *Sedum spectabile* 'Autumn Joy'
6 *Sedum maximum purpureum* ('Atropurpureum')
2 *Weigela florida* 'Purpurea'

° The National Trust can afford to be lavish with plant orders. Numbers in brackets suggest smaller quantities of plants for those who would like to economize a little and are prepared to wait.

Original design by Graham Stuart Thomas

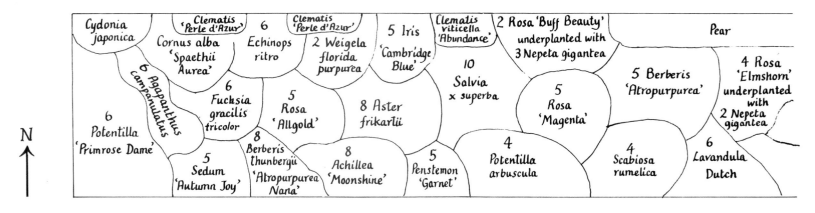

The border at Lytes Cary as it is now

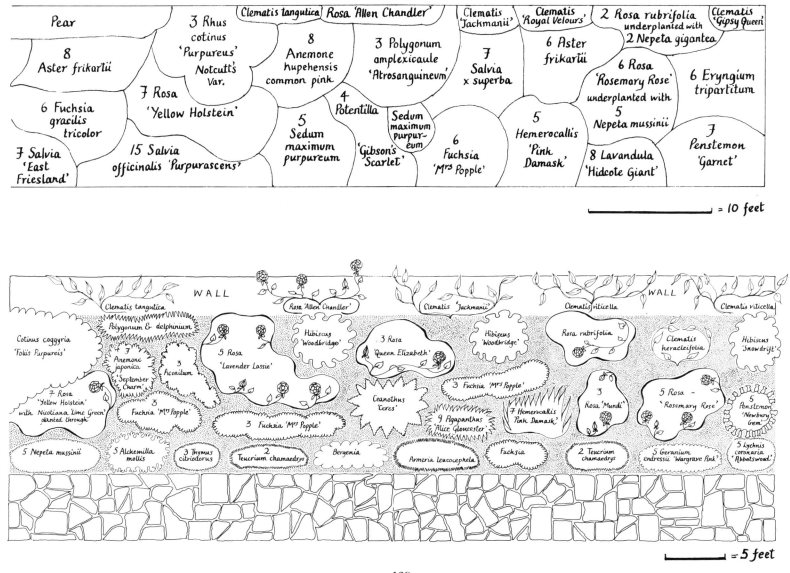

= 10 feet

= 5 feet

139

29

OLD-FASHIONED ROSES IN A MODERN PLANTING

Roses are hard to resist, especially the old-fashioned sorts, but they can be disappointing on poor soil or in wet summers. Combining them with plants which have strong foliage, as has been done here, can give the impression that roses predominate, but provides compensations when the roses are over and looks interesting even if they fail to perform properly. The twenty-foot section of border shown on the plan is part of a longer layout of double borders on either side of a grass path, punctuated by Irish yews, which stretches down to a view of the Dorset Downs. Pink shrub roses are grouped down both sides of the borders, but the ratio of roses to foliage plants everywhere is much the same as it is in the section represented, with the same sort of plants throughout. The border would probably always look better seen lengthwise rather than head on, because it is not very deep.

At the front of the bed patches of the purple bugle, the grey lamb's ear and the white-flowered *Viola cornuta* are repeated at regular intervals and the whole planting is terminated by hedges and backed by espalier apples. It would lose most of its impact without the formal straight lines which contain the loose clumps of plants and it is interesting to compare the siting of this border with the double border designed by Lanning Roper (see Chapter 16).

'Tour de Malakoff' is not a rose to attempt on thin, poor soil, but on fertile clay it will form a large bush, with stems which are not too floppy, bearing heavy purple flowers which become paler as they fade. The moss rose 'William Lobb' has a similar colouring but looks less opulent and could be a substitute in less favoured places.

The rose 'Yesterday' has the appearance of an old rose but was, in fact, raised by Harkness nursery in 1974. It flowers continuously and smells delicious, and looks the sort of rambler that might have grown in someone's grandmother's garden. 'Little White Pet' is described by Graham Stuart Thomas as 'possibly the most free flowering rose apart from the chinas' and it is hard to fault its perfect white rosette flowers.

Sambucus ebulus is the dwarf herbaceous elder. It looks much the same as the shrubby British native but dies to the ground each winter; it seems a pity not to grow something more demanding in such a good position. A more interesting plant for its place might be *Bupleurum fruticosum* which is hardy in the southern counties of England and has small greenish-yellow flowers from July until September, appearing against the bluish evergreen leaves of the shrub. This is a distinguished foliage plant which would make as much of a contribution as the other strong

OPPOSITE: *Double borders of old-fashioned roses mixed with strong foliage look full and abundant even if the flowers fail.*

background bushes like the cardoon and acanthus or the giant thistle and the fine-leaved thalictrum.

Plenty of flowers which have a long season are included for a late-summer effect. The giant scabious has pale yellow flowers and the little-known strobilanthes, which looks rather like a salvia, has purple blue ones in a similar colour range to the aconitums. The latter like a rich damp soil if they are to produce plenty of spikes. *Clematis* 'Côte d'Azur' is the herbaceous clematis which makes a clump of hyacinth-blue colour in the last months of the summer, but *Clematis* × *durandii*, a cross between a herbaceous and a shrubby clematis, might be worth considering in a similar border. It is not self-supporting but weaves its way through other plants, or can be trained up pea-sticks. The border is so full that when things like foxgloves or angelica fade, neighbouring plants including gypsophila and acanthus grow into their positions and provide the next wave of bloom. Nevertheless, it is often irresistible to add another strand of flowering.

LEFT: *'Excelsior' foxgloves hold their flowers horizontally, so that you can inspect their speckled centres.*

142

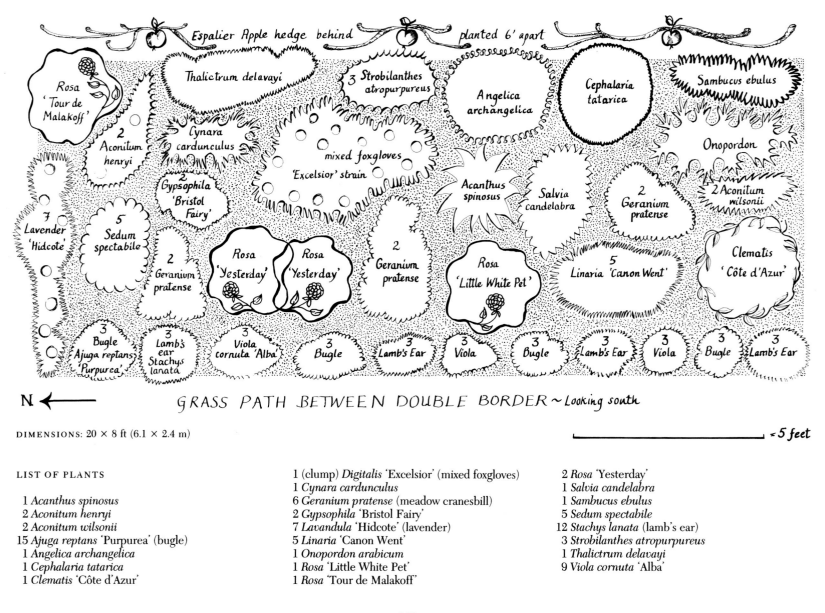

Espalier Apple hedge behind   planted 6' apart

Rosa 'Tour de Malakoff'

Thalictrum delavayi

3 Strobilanthes atropurpureus

Angelica archangelica

Cephalaria tatarica

Sambucus ebulus

2 Aconitum henryi

Cynara cardunculus

mixed foxgloves 'Excelsior' strain

Onopordon

2 Aconitum wilsonii

2 Gypsophila 'Bristol Fairy'

Acanthus spinosus

Salvia candelabra

2 Geranium pratense

7 Lavender 'Hidcote'

5 Sedum spectabile

2 Geranium pratense

Rosa 'Yesterday'

Rosa 'Yesterday'

2 Geranium pratense

Rosa 'Little White Pet'

5 Linaria 'Canon Went'

Clematis 'Côte d'Azur'

3 Bugle Ajuga reptans 'Purpurea'

3 Lamb's ear Stachys lanata

3 Viola cornuta 'Alba'

3 Bugle

3 Lamb's Ear

3 Viola

3 Bugle

3 Lamb's Ear

3 Viola

3 Bugle

3 Lamb's Ear

N ←   GRASS PATH BETWEEN DOUBLE BORDER ~ Looking south

DIMENSIONS: 20 × 8 ft (6.1 × 2.4 m)

⊢——————⊣ = 5 feet

LIST OF PLANTS

1 *Acanthus spinosus*
2 *Aconitum henryi*
2 *Aconitum wilsonii*
15 *Ajuga reptans* 'Purpurea' (bugle)
1 *Angelica archangelica*
1 *Cephalaria tatarica*
1 *Clematis* 'Côte d'Azur'

1 (clump) *Digitalis* 'Excelsior' (mixed foxgloves)
1 *Cynara cardunculus*
6 *Geranium pratense* (meadow cranesbill)
2 *Gypsophila* 'Bristol Fairy'
7 *Lavandula* 'Hidcote' (lavender)
5 *Linaria* 'Canon Went'
1 *Onopordon arabicum*
1 *Rosa* 'Little White Pet'
1 *Rosa* 'Tour de Malakoff'

2 *Rosa* 'Yesterday'
1 *Salvia candelabra*
1 *Sambucus ebulus*
5 *Sedum spectabile*
12 *Stachys lanata* (lamb's ear)
3 *Strobilanthes atropurpureus*
1 *Thalictrum delavayi*
9 *Viola cornuta* 'Alba'

143

30

WOODLAND AND WILD FLOWER BORDER

A secret path framed by dark trees leads down to a pond and a distant view. The garden which contains this vista is not large, but it has been designed by a painter and garden designer who believes that mystery and surprise are the most important elements in any garden.

The planting may look like a series of wild accidents, but is, in fact, strictly formal in design. Tall evergreens frame the woodland walk which is guarded by two rounded domes of osmanthus, whose honey-scented flowers fill the spring air. Halfway down the path four junipers mark a cross vista to a fountain, which splashes in the background as you walk towards the pond surrounded by ferns and large water-loving plants. Shade and the sound of water contribute to the feeling of coolness and tone down the bright colours of wild flowers and strong perennials like poppies. Looking back to the house in June you see a blur of wild flowers where the pinks of columbines and sweet rocket predominate. Earlier in the year, tulips followed by bluebells and irises make a different colour scheme against the permanent background of patches of purple from *Prunus cistena*, the dwarf red-leaved plum, and the purple-leaved *Viola labradorica*. Bushes of the prunus alternate with clumps of the late-flowering pink rose 'The Fairy' along both sides of the path, which may not be visible at first sight under the cloud of flowers that grow so freely throughout the borders. 'The Fairy' flowers from about the second week in July right through until the autumn and, with the purple leaves of the prunus, gives late summer colour to what is predominantly a spring border. The fact that the rose blooms rather more sparsely than it might in a flower bed with less competition from other plants does not matter in an area of garden where the impression is designed to be one of artless wilderness rather than cultivated border.

Maintenance of the borders is limited to keeping the peace between the various flowers which seed themselves everywhere. Comfrey, brunnera and the wild Welsh yellow poppy tend to dominate the gentler species like columbine and campion, but the owner takes a daily walk around his garden – even though he is now in his eighties – directing the encouragement of the weaker species and occasionally stooping to pull out a more intrusive plant himself. What looks like a state of horticultural *laissez-faire* is in reality strictly supervised. Vetch has proved a troublesome weed and frequently threatens to swamp other plants, but to the visitor who does not have to deal with the intruder it only adds to the general effect of being in a wild place full of self-sown flowers.

The evergreens framing the borders are classical in feeling, suggesting a grove rather

OPPOSITE: *A narrow path that seems almost too overgrown to walk down is mysterious and inviting.*

than a spinney. Portugal laurel, box and bay, with the occasional cypress or yew, all give the area a permanent dignity which would not have been achieved with deciduous trees and also mean that in winter the walk to the pond looks furnished and green. Some of the intermediate planting of shrubs like senecio has obviously diminished over the years, but the original design of the border was so strong that it compensates for this. The residue of earlier plantings adds character to the border rather in the same way as the deliberate odd stitch traditionally incorporated into the best Persian carpets. It could be argued that the combination of wild-looking flowers with the dark trees is prettier than a more conventional arrangement of a mixed shrub and flower border. More climbers could be grown up the evergreen framework at the back of the beds if it was felt that there was not enough floral interest after the spring flowers faded. The climbers which would be in keeping with the present scheme are species roses and clematis and perhaps more of the golden hop. Any of the 'Kiftsgate' or *Longicuspis* type roses would be in the spirit of the present mood, and so would the August-flowering *Clematis flammula* or the later *Clematis orientalis* with the lemon-yellow flowers.

The narrow path through borders with dramatically high evergreen sides creates mystery and secrecy which is what the owner likes, but as with all narrow paths – and this one is only three foot wide – it presents prob-

OPPOSITE: *Oriental poppies stand out against the dark background of a purple-leaved prunus.*

lems if the garden is much visited. This is a place to be enjoyed by the solitary walker; romance evaporates as soon as the view of another person's head and shoulders fills the vision. Two people cannot walk abreast down a path less than eight foot wide and such a width is acceptable only in much larger scale plantings. But the point of this small and intimate enclosure would be lost if the path was larger. As it is now the visitor has to walk slowly, stepping between the spreading vegetation, almost as though he were rediscovering a long-closed path in an overgrown wood.

LIST OF PLANTS

10 *Avena candida* (*Helictotrichon sempervirens*)
 2 *Buxus* 'Handsworthensis' (box)
 2 *Chamaecyparis lawsoniana* 'Fletcheri'
 1 *Cupressus macrocarpa*
 6 *Hebe pageana*
 1 *Humulus lupulus* 'Aureus' (golden hop)
 1 *Ilex × aquifolium* 'J. C. van Tol' (holly)
 4 *Juniperus* 'Skyrocket'
 1 *Laurus nobilis* (bay tree)
 2 *Osmanthus delavayi*
 1 *Paeonia lutea ludlowii* (tree peony)
 6 *Prunus × cistena*
 1 *Prunus laurocerasus* (cherry laurel)
 8 *Rosa* 'The Fairy'
 1 *Senecio greyii*
 2 *Spiraea thunbergii*
 1 *Taxus baccata* 'Fastigiata' (Irish yew)
 1 *Taxus baccata* 'Fastigiata Aureomarginata'

Underplanting and summer bedding:
    Bluebells; brunnera; campion; columbines; comfrey; ferns; honesty; *Iris xiphium*; knotweed; oriental poppies; primroses; sweet rocket; *Tellima grandiflora*; tulips; *Viola labradorica*; Welsh poppies

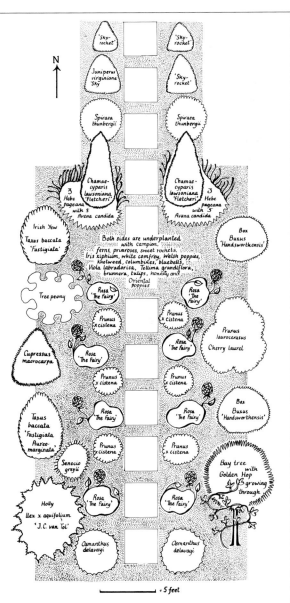

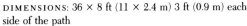

DIMENSIONS: 36 × 8 ft (11 × 2.4 m) 3 ft (0.9 m) each side of the path

147

LIST OF SUPPLIERS

IN BRITAIN

BULBS

Amand, Dutch Bulb Specialists, Clamp Hill, Stanmore, Middlesex HA7 3JS, England

Rupert Bowlby, P.O. Box 156, Kingston on Thames, Surrey, England

HERBACEOUS

Bressingham Gardens, Diss, Norfolk IP22 2AB, England

Thomas Carlile, Carlile's Corner, Twyford, Berkshire RG10 9PU, England

ROSES

David Austin Roses, Bowling Green Lane, Albrighton, Wolverhampston WV7 3HB, England

Peter Beale's Roses, London Road, Attleborough, Norfolk, England

Hillier Nurseries (Winchester) Ltd, Ampfield House, Ampfield, Romsey SO5 9PA, England

Scotts Nurseries, Merriot, Somerset TA16 5PL, England

For more sources, see *Find That Rose* published by the Rose Growers' Association, 303 Mile End Road, Colchester, Essex, England.

SEEDS

Chiltern Seeds, Bortree Stile, Ulverston, Cumbria, England

Thompson and Morgan, London Road, Ipswich IP2 0BA, England

Membership of the Hardy Plant Society (c/o Miss Barbara White, 10 St Barnabas Road, Emmer Green, Caversham, Reading RG4 8RA, England) will put you in touch with other suppliers, as will membership of the Royal Horticultural Society, Vincent Square, London SW1P 2PE, England. For details of the National Council for the Conservation of Plants and Gardens, also worth joining, contact the Royal Horticultural Society.

UNUSUAL PLANTS

Careby Manor Gardens, Careby, Stanford, Lincolnshire PE9 4EA, England

Hopleys Plants, High Street, Much Hadham, Hertfordshire SG10 6BU, England

J. and E. Parker-Jervis, Marten's Hall Farm, Longworth, Abingdon, Oxfordshire OX13 5EP (no mail order)

Unusual Plants, Beth Chatto, White Barn House, Elmstead Market, Colchester, Essex CO7 7DB, England

For more sources, see *The Plant Finder* from the Hardy Plant Society, Freepost, Worcester WR2 4BR, England

IN AMERICA (send off for price of catalogue)

HERBS

Caprilands Herb Farm, 534 Silver Street, Coventry, Connecticut 06238, USA

Sandy Mush Herb Nursery, Route # 2 Surrett Cove Road, Leicester, North Carolina 28748, USA

PERENNIALS

Bluestone Perennials, 7231 Middle Ridge, Madison, Ohio 44057, USA

Blackthorne Gardens, 48 Quincy Street, Holbrook, Massachusetts 02343–1898, USA (clematis and bulbs)

Daffodil Mart, Route 3 Box 794, Gloucester, Virginia 23061, USA

Maver Nursery, Route # 2 Box 265B, Ashville, North Carolina 28805, USA

Milaeger's Gardens, 4838 Douglas Avenue, Racine, Wisconsin 53402–2498, USA

ROSES

Jackson and Perkins Co., Box 1028, Medford, Oregon 97501, USA

Roses of Yesterday and Today, 802 Brown's Valley Road, Watsonville, California 95076–0398, USA

SEEDS

W. Atlee Burpee Co., Warminster, Pennsylvania 18974, USA

Thompson and Morgan, P.O. Box 1308, Jackson, New Jersey 08527–0308, USA

TREES, SHRUBS AND HERBACEOUS

Carroll Gardens, 444 East Main Street, Westminster, Maryland 21157, USA

Siskiyou Rare Plant Nursery, 2825 Cummings Road, Medford, Oregon 97501, USA

Wayside Gardens Co., Hodges, South Carolina 29695, USA

White Flower Farm, Route # 63, Litchfield, Connecticut 06759–0050, USA

Selected Reading

Barbara Barton, *Gardening By Mail: a Source Book* (Tusker Press, Sebastopol, California)

W. J. Bean, *Trees and Shrubs Hardy in the British Isles* (John Murray)

Beth Chatto, *The Damp Garden* (Dent)

Beth Chatto, *The Dry Garden* (Dent)

Robin Lane Fox, *Variations on a Garden* (available from R. and L. Publications Ltd, 14 Beechcroft Road, Oxford, England)

Arthur Hellyer, *The Amateur Gardener* (Collingridge)

Christopher Lloyd, *The Well-Tempered Garden* (Viking)

Brian Mathew, *The Year Round Bulb Garden* (Souvenir)

Russell Page, *The Education of a Gardener* (Penguin)

Lanning Roper, *Hardy Herbaceous Plants* (Penguin)

Graham Stuart Thomas, *Climbing Roses Old and New* (Dent)

Graham Stuart Thomas, *Old Shrub Roses* (Dent)

Graham Stuart Thomas, *Perennial Plants* (Dent)

Graham Stuart Thomas, *Shrub Roses of Today* (Dent)

CATALOGUES

Capability's Books for Gardeners, Box 114, Deer Park, Wisconsin 54007, USA

Hillier's *Manual of Trees and Shrubs* (see 'List of Suppliers' for address)

Scotts Nurseries' catalogues (see 'List of Suppliers' for address)

Almost all of the gardens can be visited through the National Gardens Scheme and are listed in their annually updated Yellow Book, *Gardens of England and Wales*, which is available from booksellers or by post from the National Gardens Scheme, 57 Lower Belgrave Street, London SW1W 0LR, England.

INDEX

Abelia × *grandiflora* 82
Abutilon suntense 102
Acanthus 20, 96, 142; *spinosus* 40, 98, 143; *perlingii* 52, 54; *capillipes* 112, 115; *palmatum* 'Dissectum' 20, 22, *platanoides* 'Globosum' 122, 125
Achillea 'Moonshine' 90, 137
Aconite 26, 66, 122, 126, 128, 134, 142
Aconitum henryi (monkshood) 111, 119, 143; *wilsonii* 143
Actinidia chinensis (kiwi fruit) 60, 64, 102
Agapanthus campanulatus 'Isis' 38, 40, 137; 'Headbourne Hybrids' 50
Ageratum 73
Ajuga pyramidalis 17; *reptans* 'Atropurpurea' 18, 19; *r.* 'Burgundy glow' (purple bugle) 14, 50, 140; *r.* 'Purpurea' 143; *r.* 'Rainbow' 115
Alchemilla mollis 22, 27, 31, 37, 50, 70, 73, 102
Allium cepa (tree onion) 37; *christophii* 17, 73, 103; *giganteum* 98; *moly* 18, 19; *ostrowskianum* 73; *rosenbachianum* 37; *roseum* 99; *schoenoprasum* (chives) 17, 37, 70, 73, 102
Aloysia citriodora 80
Alstroemeria 73
Althaea rosea (hollyhock) 47, 68
Alyssum saxatile 102
Anaphalis triplinervis 68, 119

Anchusa 'Loddon Royalist' 76, 79
Anemone 124; *hupehensis japonica* 'Honorine Joubert' 26, 27, 110, 119, 125; *h.j.* 'September Charm' 137; *japonica* 98, 116, 119; *rivularis* 54; 'St Brigid' 56
Angelica archangelica 19, 142, 143
Anthemis cupaniana 19, 59, 64, 94, 133
Anthemis nobilis (chamomile) 37; *santi-johannis* (orange daisy) 73
Anthriscus cerefolium (chervil) 17
Antirrhinum (snapdragon) 17, 37
Apple tree 126; 'Arthur Turner' 78, 79; 'Bramley' 111; 'Charles Ross' 110, 111
Aquilegia (columbine) 8, 42, 47, 68, 88, 104, 144, 147; *alpina* 90; 'McKana Hybrid' 99; 'Norah Barlow' 114, 115; *vulgaris* 102, 106
Arabis albida 'Flore Pleno' 124; *a.* 'Variegata' 37
Aralia elata (Japanese angelica tree) 94
Arisaema japonicum 55
Armeria maritima (thrift) 59
Artemisia 70, 73; *arborescens* 'Faith Raven' 82; *arbrotanum* (southernwood) 14, 17, 18, 19, 47, 45; *camphorita* 37; *canescens* 18; *dracunculus sativa* (French tarragon) 17; *lactiflora* 73; 'Lambrook Silver' 18, 19, 37;

'Margery Fish' 27; 'Powis Castle' 50, 68, 102; *schmidtiana* 64; *s.* 'Nana' 98; 'Silver Queen' 68; *stelleriana* 'Boughton' 19
Artichoke 42, 45; 'Gros Vert de Laon' 47
Asplenium scolopendrium (hart's-tongue fern) 48, 64, 86, 129
Aster (Michaelmas daisy) 45, 47, 73, 88; *acris* 73, 116, 119; *amellus* 'Nocturne' 98; 'Climax' 90; *divaricatus* (white) 47; *ericoides* 'Esther' 73; × *frikartii* 'Mönch' (blue) 47, 116, 119, 125, 134, 137; *lateriflorus* 47; 'Little Pink Lady' 119; 'Marie Ballard' 90; *thomsonii* 17
Astilbe rivularis 68, 73
Astrantia major 19, 54, 90; 'Sunningdale' 37; 'Variegata' 102
Athyrium filix-femina 'Percristatum' (fern) 52, 54; *nipponicum* 'Pictum' (fern) 54; *vidalii* (fern) 54
Atriplex halimus 64
Aubrieta 56; 'Bressingham Pink' 59; 'Dr Mules' 59
Avena candida 98, 147

Ballota acetabulosa 37, 63, 82
Baptisia australis 90, 133
Barbarea vulgaris 'Variegata' 35, 37
Beech 14, 92, 122
Begonia 130; *sutherlandii* 54

Berberis 66, 68, 70, 134; × *ottawensis* 'Purpurea' 73; *thunbergii* 'Atropurpurea Nana' 48, 94, 96, 119, 137; *t.* 'Rose Glow' 68, 133
Bergenia 96, 108; 'Ballawley' 22, 115; *stracheyi* 'Alba' 102
Blackberry 42
Blechnum penna-marina (fern) 129
Bluebell 144, 147
Borago officinalis 17
Broom 11
Brunnera 50, 130, 144, 147; 'Hadspen Cream' 133; *macrophylla* 122
Buddleia 11, 104, 122; *alternifolia* 96, 111; 'Empire Beauty' 98; *fallowiana* 'Alba' 37
Bupleurum fruticosum 10, 52, 54, 94, 140
Buxus 'Handsworthiensis' 147; latifolia maculata (golden box) 94; sempervirens 11, 14, 32, 35, 37, 42, 48, 56, 96, 98, 132; *s.* 'Suffruticosa' 19, 37, 102

Calendula officinalis (marigold) 17
Campanula 28, 125; *lactiflora* 90; *latiloba* 'Alba' 102, 124; *l.* 'Hidcote Amethyst' 124; *l.* 'High Cliffe' 124; *medium* (Canterbury bell) 90; *persicifolia* (blue) 73, 90; *p.* 'Alba' 54; *p.* 'Fleur de Neige' 31; pocharskyana 129, 133; portenschlagiana 37

Campion 144, 147
Canna iridiflora (canna lily) 70, 73
Cardamine pratensis 'Flore Pleno' (double lady's smock) 102
cardoon (*Cynara cardunculus*) 76, 142
Carpenteria californica 37, 64, 82
Catananche caerulea (white) 125
Ceanothus 11, 122, 134; × 'Autumnal Blue' 64, 102; 'Delight' 24; × 'Gloire de Versailles' 64; *impressus* 22; 48, 50; 'Repens' 68; *thyrsiflorus* 24, 122; 'Trewithen Blue' 82
Cedar 130
Cephalaria tatarica 143
Cerastium tomentosum (snow-in-summer) 64, 86
Ceratostigma willmottianum 125
Chamaecyparis lawsoniana 'Fletcheri' 147; *l.* 'Witzeliana' 40; *obtusa* 'Crippsii' 115; *pisifera* 'Boulevard' 112, 115
Chard 19
Cheiranthus 130; 'Bowles Mauve' 50, 60, 63, 64, 100, 102; *cheiri* (wallflower) 37, 42, 100; 'Harpur Crewe' 50, 102; 'Moonlight' 133; 'Wenlock Beauty' 102
Cherry 66, 92, 126
Chestnut tree 126
Chionodoxa luciliae 106, 124, 129
Choisya ternata 22, 37, 32, 94

Chrysanthemum balsamita 37; *haradjani* 24, 35; Korean 68; 'Mawi' 18; *parthenium* (feverfew) 17; *p.* 'Rowallane' 54; *rubellum* 'Clara Curtis' 47, 68; *uliginosum* 119; 'Wirral Supreme' 47, 106
Cirsium rivulare 60, 64
Cistus 76, 79, 80, 82; × *aguilari* 'Maculatus' 79; × *corbariensis* 79, 82; *ladanifer* 22, 40, 82; × *laurifolius* 76, 79; × *purpureus* 79; 'Silver Pink' 18, 102
Clematis 24, 28, 60, 73; *alpina* 'Columbine' 64; *a.* 'Frances Rivis' 82; *a.* 'Ruby' 64, 82; *a.* 'Willy' 82; 'Beauty of Worcester' 102; 'Côte d'Azur' 142, 143; × *durandii* 90; 102, 142; × *eriostemon* 'Hendersonii' 90; 'Etoile Rose' 64, 82, 102; *flammula* 116, 147; *grewiiflora* 64; 'Gypsy Queen' 73, 137; *integrifolia* 115; 'Jackmanii Alba' 137; 'Jackmanii superba' 26, 27, 79, 102; 'Markham's Pink' 64; *montana* 60; 'Mrs Spencer Castle' 133; *orientalis* 82, 147; 'Perle d'Azur' 137; *rehderana* 64, 80, 82; 'Royal Velours' 137; 'Rubra' 102; *tangutica* 137; *viticella* 54, 104; *v.* 'Abundance' 137; *v.* 'Alba Luxurians' 64; *v.* 'Rubra' 19
Cleome 11
Clerodendrum trichotomum 98
Colchicum 'Princess Astrid' 64; *speciosum* 'Album' 64, 104
Comfrey 144, 147
Conifer 80, 83, 112
Convolvulus 10; *cneorum* 24, 27
Cornflower 42, 45, 47
Cornus alba 'Elegantissima 50; *a.* 'Spaethii Aurea' 137; *mas* (cornelian cherry) 50; *m.* 'Variegata' 32, 37
Cosmos 11, 45, 47; *atrosanguineus* 106; *bipinnatus* 104
Cotinus 66, 92; *coggygria* 'Foliis Purpureis' 20, 22, 68, 73, 94, 137
Cotoneaster horizontalis 'Variegatus' 50, 94; × *waterii* 38, 40, 50
Courgette 14, 17, 18
Crambe cordifolia 66, 70, 76, 78, 79, 88, 90, 104, 106
Cranesbill 20, 22, 45, 66, 88, 130
Crepis incana 63, 64

Crocosmia 'Citronella' 119; *masonorum* 19, 119
Crocus sieberi 56; *speciosus* 37; *tomasinianus* 129
Cuphea cyanea 'Firefly' 73
Cupressus macrocarpa 147
Curtonus paniculatus 37
Cyclamen 60, 126, 128; *coum* 66, 129; *hederifolium* 64, 66, 82, 129
Cydonia japonica (flowering quince) 137
Cynara cardunculus 143
Cypress 38, 40, 112
Cyrtomium (fern) 54
Cytisus battandieri 22, 102; × *praecox* 102

Daffodil 114, 126
Daisy 8, 10, 42, 45, 73, 116
Dahlia 11, 104, 122; 'Bishop of Llandaff' 45, 47; 'Fascination' 50
Daphne 26, 45; *laureola* 37; *mezereum* 47; *m. alba* 60, 64; 'Somerset' 64
Delphinium 14, 45, 47, 88, 116, 134; *belladonna hybrid* 47; 'Pacific Hybrid' 19, 90, 119
Deutizia × *elegantissima* 40; monbeigii 79
Dianthus 58; *deltoides* 31, 59; 'Doris' 59; 'Frank's Frilly' 112, 115; 'Mrs Sinkins' 45, 47, 68; 'Prudence' 59; 'White Ladies' 27, 59; 'Widdicombe Fair' 98
Diascia rigescens 73, 100, 102
Dicentra spectabilis 'Alba' 102
Dictamnus fraxinella 'Purpureus' 91
Digitalis (foxglove) 13, 17, 48, 50, 79, 130, 142; 'Excelsior' 142, 143; 'Foxy' 19; × *mertonensis* 50; *purpurea* 19, 50, 73
Doronicum 130; 'Miss Mason' 133
Dorycnium suffruticosum hirsutum 68
Dryopteris filix-mas (fern) 52, 54; *polystichum aculcatum* 129

Echinops ritro 137
Echium 'Blue Bedder' 88, 91
Elaeagnus × *ebbingei* 94
Epimedium × *versicolor* 'Alba' 54
Eranthis × 'Guinea Gold' (aconite) 129; *hyemalis* 129
Eremurus robustus (foxtail lily) 73

Erigeron glaucus 98
Erodium chrysanthemum 112, 115
Eryngium 70; *alpinum* 98; × *oliverianum* 73; *planum* 91; *tripartitum* 137; *variifolium* 17
Escallonia 'Iveyi' 48, 50
Espalier apple 42, 140; 'Orleans Reinette' 14; 'Red Melba' 19; 'Tydeman's Late Orange' 14; 'Wagener' 14, 19
Euonymus 'Macrophyllus Albus' 48
Eupatorium purpureum 68
Euphorbia 38, 108, 130; *dulcis* 82, 98; *polychroma* 102, 106; *robbiae* 37, 94, 133; *wulfenii* 22, 40, 104, 106, 110, 133

Fatsia japonica 104
Felicia amelloides (blue Africa daisy) 14, 17, 52
Fern 28, 84, 86, 96, 128, 130, 144, 147
ferula communis (fennel) 32, 37; *c. purpurea* 37
Filipendula hexapetala (dropwort) 37, 124
Flax, *see Linum narbonense*
Foeniculum vulgare purpureum (fennel) 19, 102
Fragaria vesca 'Baron Solemacher' 68, 86
Fritillaria imperialis (crown imperial) 42, 47, 68, 108, 111; *meleagris* 55; *pontica* 55; *pyrenaica* 114, 115
Fuchsia 28, 122, 134; 'Army Nurse' 98; *gracilis tricolor* 137; *magellanica* 'Alba' 125; *m.* 'Versicolor' 98; 'Mrs Popple' 40, 137; 'Riccartonii' 68

Galanthus caucasicus 129; *elwesii* (snowdrop) 37, 80, 112, 114, 115, 128, 129; *plicatus* 'Warham' 55
Galega officinalis 119
Galtonia candicans 91
Garrya elliptica 48, 50
Gaura lindheimeri 91
Genista tinctoria (dyer's greenweed) 32, 37
Geranium 11, 80, 83; 'Claridge Druce' 102; *collinum* 79; *endressii* 'Wargrave Pink' 22, 37, 68, 111; 'Johnson's Blue 22, 31, 102, 111, 119; *lancastriense* 86;

macrorrhizum 68, 102; *maderense* 17, 19; *phaeum* 'Album' 106; *pratense* 143; *procurrens* 76, 79, *psilostemon* 17, 18, 91; *rectum* 'Album' 19, *renardii* 106; 'Russell Prichard' 22, 73; *sanguineum* 'Album' 102; *s. lancastriense* 17, 98; *wallichianum* 'Buxton's Blue' 76, 124, 125
Geum 'Mrs Bradshaw' 91
Gillenia trifoliata 17, 18; *byzantinus* 91
Gladiolus 'The Bride' 18
Grasses 96
Gypsophila 'Bristol Fairy' 142, 143; *paniculata* 'Rosy Veil' 17, 78, 79

Heather 48
Hebe albicans 110, 111; × *andersonii* 82; *armstrongii* 82; 'Cranleigh Gem' 64; *pagiana* 83, 147; *pinguifolia* 'Pagei' 64; *subalpina* 104, 108, 110, 111
Hedera colchica 'Dentata Variegata' 37, 82, 83; 'Glymii' 94; *helix* (common ivy) 24, 32, 50, 80, 82, 84, 126; *h.* 'Arborescens' 37; *h. canariensis* 'Glacier' 82; *h.* 'Gloire de Marengo' 83; *hibernica* 82, 83
Helenium autumnale 'Bruno' 119; *a.* 'The Bishop' 119; *a.* 'Moerheim Beauty' 119; *rubrum* (bronze) 119
Helianthemum 56, 58; 'Ben Hope' 59; 'Miss Mellish' 119; 'The Bride' 27, 37, 59; 'Wisley Primrose' 64
Helichrysum angustifolium (curry plant) 27, 98, 102; *macrophyllum* 98; *serotinum* 65
Helleborus 24, 84, 108, 126, 128; *corsicus* 27, 40, 48, 50, 106; *foetidus* 37, 129; *lividus* 'Boughton Beauty' 27; 'Nigristern' 52, 54; *orientalis* 52, 54, 110, 111, 112, 115, 128, 129; *o. guttatus* 86
Hemerocallis (day lily) 22, 28, 38, 137; *flava* 91; 'Pink Damask' 137; 'Whichford' 54
Heracleum mantegazzianum (hogweed) 94
Heuchera americana 115
Hibiscus 134; *syriacus* 'Blue Bird' 37, 40
Holcus mollis 'Variegata' 106
Hosta 96, 108, 114, 128, 130;

albomarginata 19, 102; *elata* 129; *fortunei* 'Albopicta' 18, 54, 129, 133; *plantaginea* 115; *sieboldiana* 54, 102, 110, 129; *undulata* 115; *ventricosa* 129
House leek 80, 83
Humulus lupulus 'Aureus' (golden hop) 147
Hydrangea arborescens 'Grandiflora' 54; 'Grandiflora' 130, 133; 'Lanarth White' 73, 94; *macrophylla* 'Beauté Vendômoise' 54; 'Mariesii' 52, 54; *paniculata* 'Grandiflora' 96; *preziosa* 73; 'Quadricolor' 52, 54; 'Tricolor' 52; *villosa* 22
Hypericum × *moseranum* 'Tricolor' 50; *olympicum* 'Citrinum' 58
Hyssop (dwarf) 122, 125
Hyssopus officinalis 37

Iberis sempervirens (candytuft) 47, 56, 59
Ilex (holly) 100; 'Amber' 48; 'Golden Queen' 32, 37; × *aquifolium* 'J.C. van Tol' 48, 147
Indigolfera kirilowi 10, 70, 73
Inula helenium 88, 91
Iris 28, 38, 96, 110, 122, 130, 134, 144; 'Cambridge Blue' 137; 'Cliffs of Dover' 111; *foetidissima* 'Variegata' 133; *germanica* 98; *histrioides* 56, 115; *kaempferi* 28, 31; *laevigata* 'Alba' 28, 31; 'Mission Ridge' 124; *pallida* 124; *p.* 'Dalmatica' 31, 98, 124; *p.* 'Jane Phillips' 27, 47, 79; *p.* 'Aurea Variegata' 106; *p.* 'Variegata' 65; *pseudacorus* 28; *reticulata* 56; *sibirica* 28, 106; *s.* 'Caesar' (dark blue) 106; *unguicularis* 'Mary Barnard' 60, 65; 'White City' 111; *xiphium* 147

Jasmine 24, 60, 80
Jasminum nudiflorum 60, 65, 82; *officinale* 'Affine' 82; *revolutum* 37
Jonquil 114
Juniper 24, 66, 144
Juniperus 'Pfitzerana' 102, 108; *sabina tamariscifolia* 27; *virginiana* 'Skyrocket' 68, 102, 147

Kerria japonica 37, 82

151

Kniphofia (red hot poker) 92; 'Atlanta' 91; 'Corallina' 94; 'Underway' 94; 'Royal Standard' 94;
Knotweed 147
Kolkwitzia amabilis 66, 68

Lactuca plumieri 91
Lamium 'Beacon Silver' 68; *maculatum* 'Nancy's White' 54, 65; *m.* 'Roseum' 98; *orvala* (giant dead nettle) 106
Lasiogrostis splendens 98
Lathraea clandestina 73
Lathyrus latifolius albus 91; *odoratus* 'Painted Lady' 47; 'Rose Queen' 65; *tuberosus* (sweet pea) 11, 88, 91; *vernus* 106; *v.* 'Roseus' 114, 115
Laurel 126
Lauristinus 'Eve Price' 98
Laurus nobilis (bay tree) 147
Lavender 10, 56, 108, 116
Lavandula 'Hidcote Giant' 137; 'Loddon Pink' 98; *spica* 'Hidcote' 27, 65, 110, 111, 143; *vera* (Dutch lavender) 119, 137
Lavatera 'Mont Blanc' 35, 37; 'Silver Cup' 98, 99
Leucanthemum vulgare (ox-eye daisy) 68
Leucojum aestivum 124; *vernum* 'Warham' (snowflake) 55
Liatris spicata alba 125
Libertia ixioides 73; *peregrina* 70, 73
Lithospermum 'Grace Ward' 59
Lychnis flos-cuculi (white ragged robin) 124
Lilium regale 17, 18, 19, 27; *szovitsianum* 128, 129; *tigrinum* 'Splendens' (tiger lilies) 114, 115; *speciosum* 'Rubrum' 27
Lily 50, 79, 96, 126, 128
Limonium latifolium 'Violetta' 18; *sinuatum* 98
Linaria 'Canon Went' 143
Linum narbonense (flax) 30, 31, 119, 122; *rubrum* (red flax) 73
Lithospermum 'Grace Ward' 59
Lonicera 56; × *americana* 65; *ciliosa* 126, 129; *etrusca* (honeysuckle) 13, 26, 60, 65; *fragrantissima* 80, 82; *japonica* 'Aureoreticulata' 54; *j.* 'Aureo-variegata' 37; *nitida* 'Baggesen's Gold' 20, 22, 88, 92, 94; 'Serotina' 102; *syringantha* 102; *tragophylla* 126

Love-in-a-mist 45, 47
Lunaria annua (honesty) 50, 99, 147; *a.* 'Variegata' 37, 54, 114, 115; *a.* 'Variegata Alba' 55
Lupinus 'Russell Hybrids' (lupin) 98, 99
Lychnis chalcedonica 91; *coronaria* 'Alba' 35, 37, 106
Lysimachia ciliata 110, 111, 119; *clethroides* (loosestrife) 54, 108; *nummularia* (creeping jenny) 94; *punctata* 110, 111
Lythrum salicaria 'Brightness' 119; *s.* 'Robert' 98

Macleaya cordata (plume poppy) 28
Magnolia 84
Mahonia 104; *aquifolium* 'Undulata' 129
Malus robusta (crab apple) 92, 94
Malva alcea 'Fastigiata' 98; *moschata* (white mallow) 103; 'Primley Blue' (mallow) 47
Mandragora officinarum (mandrake) 37
Marguerite 66
Marigold 14
Marrubium incanum 63, 65
Matthiola 'White Perennial Stock' 47
Meadowsweet 125
Meconopsis (poppy) 42, 144
Meconopsis cambrica 'Welsh poppy' 18, 19, 144, 147 (*see* Shirley poppy)
Mentha × *gentilis* 'Variegata' (Scotch mint) 17; × *rotundifolia variegata* 50, 94
Miscanthus sinensis 'Silver feather' 73
Muscari (grape hyacinth) 73; *armeniacum* 'Album' 124; 'Blue Spike' 124
Monarda 96; *didyma* 'Cambridge Scarlet' 17; *d.* 'Croftway Pink' 119; 'Prairie Night' 98
Montbretia 134
Morina longiflora 20, 60
Moss 84
Myosotis alpestris 124; *sylvatica* (forget-me-not) 32, 37, 73

Narcissus 68, 115, 128; × *accidentalis* 55; 'Cedric Morris' 114; *cyclamineus* 129; 'Dove Wings' 55; *minor* 114; *triandrus* 40, 129

Nasturtium 116
Nepeta 96; 'Blue Beauty' 98; *faassenii* 98; *gigantea* 137; *mussinii* (catmint) 19, 68, 119, 122, 137; *m.* 'Improved' 98, 99; 'Six Hills Giant' 65, 91, 110, 111; 'Souvenir d'André Chaudron' 47; 'Valerie Finnis' 98
Nerine bowdenii 65, 82
Nicotiana 35, 100, 130; *affinis* 78, 91, 98, 99, 103; *langsdorffii* 106; *sylvestris* 11, 37, 50, 73, 78, 80, 106
Nymphaea (waterlily) 28; *caroliniana nivea* 30; *lactea* 30; × 'Laydekeri purpurata' 30; 'Rose Nymph' 30, 31; 'Sunrise' 30, 31
Nyssas 92

Ocimum basilicum (basil) 17
Oenothera biennis (evening primrose) 119; *missouriensis* 103; *trichocalyx* 80
Olearia × *scilloniensis* 37
Omphalodes 63, 65; *cappadocica* 'Blue-eyed Mary' 133
Onopordon arabicum (giant thistle) 76, 78, 79, 88, 91, 142, 143
Origanum vulgare (marjoram) 18; *v.* 'Aureum' (golden) 37, 100, 110
Osmanthus delavayi 48, 54, 144, 147
Osteospermum 100; 'Buttermilk' 83; *ecklonis* 82, 85, 103

Paeonia 8, 20, 22, 32, 37, 42, 45, 68, 96, 104, 108; 'Bowl of Beauty' 68; *delavayi* 115; 'Duchesse de Nemours' 18, 19; 'Kelways Glorious' 47; *lutea ludlowii* 20, 22, 28, 147; *obovata alba* 106; *officinalis* 22, 47, 91; *o.* 'Alba Plena' 110; *o.* 'Rubra' 37, 116, 119; *suffruticosa* (white) 103; *s.* 'Sakurajashi' 68
Panicum virgatum 'Rubrum' 98
Papaver orientale 'Marcus Perry' 88, 91, 122, 147; *somniferum* 91, 99
Parahebe catarractae 'Alba' 37
Parthenocissus henryana 82; *inserta* (virginia creeper) 70, 73
Pear 42, 130; 'Beurre Hardy' 110, 111; 'Conference' 47; 'William's Bon Chrétien' 47
Pelargonium crispum 83; *graveolens* 83; *tomentosum* 83

Penstemon 24; 'Apple Blossom' 98; 'Garnet' 17, 27, 137; 'Sour Grapes' 18; 'True Blue' 17
Petroselenum crispum (parsley) 37
Petunia 35, 37, 100, 132; *hybrida* (white petunia) 103
Philadelphus 'Aureus' 130; *coronarius* 'Aureus' 133; *virginal* 86
Phlomis italica (pink sage) 65; *russeliana* 94
Phlox maculata 'Old Rectory White' 54; *paniculata* 73, 103; *p.* 'Fujiyama' 119; *p.* 'Hampton Court' 19; *p.* 'Mother of Pearl' 119; *p.* subulata 'G. F. Wilson' 59
Phygelius aequalis 'Yellow Trumpet' 54, 83
Pinus mugo (mountain pine) 70, 73, 96
Piptanthus laburnifolius 82
Pittosporum 'Garnettii' 48, 50
Platycodon grandiflorum 124
Poached egg flower 47
Polemonium (Jacob's Ladder) 37, 130; *caeruleum* 133; *c.* 'Richardsonii' 88, 91
Polygonatum canaliculatum (Solomon's seal) 54; *amplexicaule* 91; *a.* 'Atrosanguineum' 137; *campanulatum* 98
Polypodium 'Cambricum' 129; *vulgare* 86
Potentilla alba 59, 122, 125; *arbuscula* 137; 'Gibson's Scarlet' 137; 'Kathleen Dykes' 40; 'Longacre' 59; 'Mandschurican' 124; *nitida* 'Rubra' 59; 'Primrose Dame' 137; *veitchii* 37
Primrose 130, 147
Primula 115; 'Gold Lace' 130, 133; *veris* (cowslip) 130, 133; *vulgaris* 'Marie Crousse' 133; *v.* 'Alba Plena' 133
Privet 130
Prunella webbiana 'Alba' 27
Prunus × *cistena* 144, 147; *laurocerasus* 147; *l.* 'Otto Luyken' 129; *l.* 'Zabeliana' 115; *sargentii* 66, 68; *subhirtella* 'Autumnalis' 68, 104; 'Tai-Haku' (cherry tree) 19; *tenella* 122; *t.* 'Fire Hill' 108, 110, 111
Pulmonaria azurea 'Munstead Blue' 110; *officinalis* 98, 108; *saccharata* (lungwort) 86

Pyracantha 20; 'Orange Glow' 22

Quickthorn 56

Rehmannia guttata 19
Reseda lutea (giant mignonette) 91
Rhododendron 10
Rhubarb 42; 'Cawood Castle' 47, 88
Rhus 70, 92, 134
Ribes 'Albescens' (flowering currant) 106, 122
Robinia 'Frisia' 20, 22; *kelseyi* 126, 128; *pseudoacacia* 'Frisia' 50
Rosa 24, 26, 28, 45, 60, 66, 68, 73, 96, 100, 104, 140; 'Alba' 111; *alba* 'Celeste' 68; *alexandra* 82; 'Allen Chandler' 137; 'Allgold' 137; 'Aloha' 24, 27, 84, 86, 103; 'Altissimo' 68; 'Anna Louisa' 27; 'Apricot Silk' 27; Bourbon 42; 'Buff Beauty' 110, 137; *californica* 'Plena' 110, 111; 'Cardinal Richelieu' 27; *centifolia* 'de Meaux' 102; 'Cerise Bouquet' 108, 110; 'Chapeau de Napoléon' 73; 'Charles de Mills' 83, 86; 'Claire Jacquier' 27; 'Complicata' (gallica) 100, 102; 'Comte de Chambord' 84, 86; 'Constance Spry' 86; 'Cornelia' 22, 116, 118, 119; 'de Resht' 100, 103; 'Elmshorn' 137; 'Empress Josephine' 103; 'F. J. Grootendorst' 98; 'Fantin Latour' 100, 110, 111; 'Fountains' 66; 'Frances E. Lester' 111, 126, 129; 'Frau Dagmar Hastrup' 111; 'Frensham' 91; 'Fritz Nobis' 47; 'Golden Showers' 130, 133; 'Goldfinch' 14, 19; 'Grüss an Aachen' 73; 'Iceberg' 84, 86, 111, 122, 124; 'Karlsruhe' 103; 'Kathleen Harrop' 40, 103; 'Kiftsgate' 126, 147; 'La Reine Victoria' 47; 'Little White Pet' 140, 143; *longicuspis* 37, 147; 'Magenta' 137; 'May Queen' 54; 'Mme Alfred Carrière' 24, 27; 'Mme Isaac Pereire' 47, 68; 'Mme Pierre Oger' 47; *moyesii* 70, 98, 112; 'Mrs Lester' 126; 'Mundi' 134; 'Nevada' 111; 'New Dawn' 60, 65, 103; 'Nuits de Young' 119; *pendulina* 112, 115; 'Penelope' 27; 'Petite Hollande' 100, 102, 103; *primula* 80, 82; 'Queen of Holland' 111; 'Raubritter' 103; 'Rosemary Rose'

137; 'Roseraie de l'Hay' 66, 68; *rubiginosa* (sweetbriar) 40, 80, 82; *rubrifolia* 40, 66, 68, 92, 94, 98, 103, 137; *rugosa* 66, 110; *r.* 'Blanc Double de Coubert' 98; *r.* 'Souvenir de Philémon Cochet' 86, 111; 'Sammy' 119; 'The Alchemist' 84, 86; 'The Fairy' 68, 102, 103, 144, 147; 'Thisbe' 119; 'Tour de Malakoff' 140, 143; 'Tuscany' 98; 'White Wings' 68; 'Wickwar' (souleiana hybrid) 37; 'Wilhelm' 119; 'William Lobb' 68, 140; 'Yellow Holstein' 137; 'Yesterday' 140, 143; 'Zéphirine Drouhin' 24, 27
Rosmarinus 'Benenden Blue' 79; 'Blue Spire' 76; 'Cypriot' 79; *officinalis* 10, 68; *o.* 'Miss Jessup's Upright' 94; 'Severn Sea' 103
Ruscus aculeatus (butcher's broom) 129
Rumex acetosa (sorrel) 18, 37
Runner bean 19
Ruta graveolens 'Jackman's Blue' (rue) 18, 35, 37, 108, 111, 122, 125

salix alba 'Argentea' (willow) 10, 63, 70, 73; × *balfourii* 112, 115; *fargesii* 112, 115
Salvia 48, 73, 82, 122, 134, 142; *argentea* 65; *candelabra* 143; 'East Friesland' 137; *farinacea* 'Blue Bedder' 18; *grahamii* 19; *guaranitica* 83; *haematodes* 17, 18; *horminum* 19; involucrata 'Bethelli' 17, 18; *leucantha* 19; *nemerosa*

superba 'Lubeca' 17, 18, 73; *neurepia* 17, 18; *officinalis* (Barnsley House narrow leaf version) 37; *o.* (culinary sage) 18; *o.* 'Icterina' 18, 50, 94; *o.* 'Purpurascens' 27, 37, 50, 66, 68, 106, 137; *o.* 'Tricolor' 18; *patens* 18, 73; × *superba* 137; *transcaucasica* 17; *turkestanica* 17
Salvium horminum (clary) 17, 88, 91
sambucus aurea 'Aureomarginata' 130, 133; *ebulus* 140, 143; *nigra* 'Albovariegata' (elder) 10, 37, 94; *n.* 'Aurea' 32, 50
Sanguinaria canadensis 'Flore Pleno' 54
Sanguisorba minor (salad burnet) 35, 37
Santolina 50; *incana* 22, 35, 103; *virens* 48, 50
Saponaria officinalis 59
Satureja hortensis (summer savory) 17; *montana* (winter savory) 37
Scabiosa caucasica 125; *rumelica* 47, 134, 137
Scabious (giant) 142
Scilla 114, 115, 128; *bifolia* 129; *tubergeniana* 129
Sedum album (stonecrop) 30, 31; 'Autumn Joy' 47, 91, 104, 106, 111, 136, 137; *maximum purpureum* 137; 'Ruby Glow' 73; *spectabile* 143
Sempervivum 30
Senecio 108; *cineraria* 27; *greyi* 111, 147; *leucostachys* 82, 83; *laxifolius* 84, 86, 94; *monroi* 65; *reinoldi* 65
Shirley poppy 45, 47

Sidalcea 'Sussex Beauty' 119
Silene maritima 65; *m.* 'Rosea' 98; 'Richmond' 108, 111; *schafta* 'Abbotswood' 58
Sisyrinchium angustifolium 28, 30, 31, 76; *striatum* 27, 79
Skimmia japonica 'Fragrans' 129
Solanum crispum 'Alba' 65; *jasminoides* 'Album' 82
sorbus aria 'Lutescens' (whitebeam) 94
spartium junceum 96
Sphaeralcea munroana 82, 83
Spiraea 32, 66, 88; 'Anthony Waterer' 68, 119; × *arguta* 22, 86, 88, 91, 106; × *bumalda* 'Goldflame' 20, 22, 94; *thunbergii* 147; × *vanhoutei* 37
St John's wort 58
Stachys lanata 14, 17, 18, 19, 22, 108, 111, 140, 143; *l.* 'Silver Carpet' 65
Stephanandra incisa 40
Stock 40
Strobilanthes 142
Sweet rocket 144, 147
Sweet William 8, 42, 45, 47
Symphoricarpos orbiculatus 'Compactum' 94; *o.* 'Varieagatus' 94
Symphytum × *uplandicum* 91
Syringa (lilac) 70, 82; Afghanica 65; 'Mme Lemoine' 73; *vulgaris* 'Firmament' 48, 50

Tanacetum vulgare 18
Taxus baccata (yew) 10, 11, 13, 32, 37, 70, 80, 82, 84, 96; *b.* 'Fastigiata' 140, 147; *b.* 'Fastigiata Aureomarginata' 147

Tellima grandiflora 19, 147
Teucrium chamaedrys (germander) 37, 82, 98; *fruticans* 82
Thalictrum aquilegifolium 18, 37, 106; *delavayi* 142, 143; *speciosissimum* 91
Thermopsis caroliniana 114, 115
Thuya occidentalis 'Rheingold' 112, 115
Thymus 79, 82; × *citriodorus* 'Aureus' 37; × *c.* 'Silver Queen' 59, 65; *doerfleri* 37; *vulgaris* (thyme) 18, 35, 37, 58, 59, 79
Tiarella cordifolia 40, 54
Tradescantia andersoniana 'J. C. Weguelin' 27; 'Osprey' 91; *virginiana* 19
Tricyrtis hirtis 'Alba' 55
Trillium grandiflorum 55
Tropaeolum canariense 11; *majus* (nasturtium) 73
Tulipa 37, 42, 73, 100, 133, 144, 147; 'Artist' 103; 'Clara Butt' 47, 68; *clusiana* 56; *c. chrysantha* 99; 'Empress of India' 59; 'General de Wet' 47; 'Greenland' 103; 'Orange Favourite' 73; 'Peach Blossom' 47; *praestans* 56; *p.* 'Fusilier' 99; 'Rembrandt' 68; *turkestanica* 99

Ulmus × *sarniensis* 'Dicksonii' 70, 73

Valerian 28
Verbascum (mullein) 30, 50; 'Broussa' 50; *olympicum* 27; *vernale* 31

Verbena 73; *bonariensis* 70, 73, 98; *rigida* 18, 79, 99
Veronica 28; *gentianoides* 106
Vetch 144
Viburnum × *bodnantense* 38, 40; *carlcephalum* 40, 63, 65; *opulus* 38, 40; *o.* 'Compactum' 98, 99; 'Xanthocarpum' (guelder rose) 92, 94; *tinus* (lauristinus) 94
Vinca major 'Variegata' 94, 133; *minor* (lesser periwinkle) 86
Vine 82
viola 45, 56, 58, 68, 110; *cornuta* 111, 122; *c.* 'Alba' 73, 115, 140, 143; *c.* 'Belmont Blue' 59; 'Bowles Black' 31, 47; 'Huntercombe purple' 47; 'Jackanapes' 59; *labradorica* 59, 144, 147; 'Little David' 55; 'Little Dawn' 55; 'Maggie Mott' 124, 125, 133; *odorata* 115; *o.* 'Aurea' 55, 73; *septentrionalis* 54; *tricolor* (heartsease) 59; × *wittrockiana* 'Sunny Boy' (yellow) 18; × *w.* 'Ullswater' (blue) 18, 88, 91
Violet 82
Vitis 'Brant' 83

Weigela (variegated) 70; *florida* 'Foliis Purpureis' 96, 99; *f.* 'Purpurea' 137; 'Newport Red' 66, 68
Willow 112
Wisteria sinensis 24, 27; *s.* 'Alba' 65, 124; *venusta* 122, 124

Yucca gloriosa 'Variegata' 73